The Hidden History of SACRAMENTO BASEBALL

MARSHALL P. GARVEY

The Hidden History of

SACRAMENTO BASEBALL

The Events
and Players That
Have Made the River City a Baseball Heaven
from 1860 to the Present Day

ISBN: 978-0-578-49354-1

Front cover design by Wordzworth

First printing edition 2019

Printed by Amazon KDP

To my loving family: parents Bill and Bonnie, sisters
Morgan and Kira, and brother Nick. Your tireless love,
input and support made my dream come true.

To my Last Token Gaming friends and colleagues: Terry Randolph,
Isaac Smith, Jake Rushing, Michael Ros, Kazuo Koyama, Michael
Mygind, Sean Willis, Brian McKelvey, Alex Aguilar, Ben Fitzgerald,
Dave De Leon, and Sigi Cardenas. I wouldn't have grown as a writer
without collaborating the past six years with you all. You're the best.

To my late writing heroes, Roger Ebert and Jimmy Breslin.
You inspired me to write at a high level in my formative years
at the keyboard, and I wish you were both here to read this.

To Greg Voelm, who gave a soon-to-be UC Davis graduate the
dream job of a lifetime by assigning this book in June 2014.

To the 2017 Los Angeles Dodgers. They didn't win it all, but they
saved me from rock bottom. I'll never forget that. They were the
best, and deserved better than to be cheated out of a title.

To Todd in the Shadows. Your videos made for good
company and laughter during this long process.

And most of all, to my inspiration as a history writer, Rick
Perlstein. It was back in the magical summer of 2013, perusing my
grandmother's copy of *Nixonland*, that I became determined to
write history on a large scale one day. This is just the first step.

TABLE OF CONTENTS

INTRODUCTION

One of the endearing components of baseball is how fascinating it is at the regional level. Given it's the national pastime, many examine the game's history primarily through that lens, myself being no exception. I consider studying MLB history tantamount to transcribing the Dead Sea Scrolls, every team, executive, coach and player creating a rich tapestry that must be memorized and passed down to others accordingly.

Yet while it's fun to get caught up in the mystique of the game's most widely recognized moments and figures, it's even more fun to observe its happenings in specific states and cities. If anything, it's necessary to paint a full picture. After all, even the most esteemed Hall of Famers and championship teams started as kids in a sandlot and minor league teams of obscure renown. Baseball is a sport that can spontaneously and organically happen in any place, thus enabling its magic to proliferate boundlessly.

This project is special to me, as my time living in Sacramento is commensurate with my time as a baseball fan. I moved to the River City with my family in May 2000, the same year I started to become obsessed with the finest sport in the world at age ten. It was that same year that marked the inaugural season of the Sacramento River Cats, and during my first game at Raley Field that summer I discovered the Minnesota Twins while flipping through a program, thus finding my childhood team.

However, even as I followed the game with bottomless passion and studied its history year after year, I remained strangely oblivious to the local history that preceded the River Cats. I was aware that some elite players hailed from here, most eminently Larry Bowa and Steve Sax. But I knew nothing about the Altas, the Gilt Edge, the Senators and Solons, or that the Target on Broadway used to be a heralded baseball stadium. I didn't know that long before any major league team called California its home, Sacramento pioneered the game's growth in the state for a full century.

Fortunately, that all changed in June 2014. With my graduation from UC Davis imminent, I was desperately looking for history-related work, knowing my B.A. in history wasn't likely to yield too many options. I submitted my writing credentials to the Sacramento County Historical Society, and just a week or two before my cap-and-gown ceremony I was summoned to a meeting at a coffee place in Carmichael.

Waiting for me were then-SCHS president Greg Voelm and local baseball historian Alan O'Connor. As one of my writing samples was an amateur baseball article (about the value of Clayton Kershaw's then-new contract with the Los Angeles Dodgers), Voelm proposed a project: a new book about the history of baseball in Sacramento, including a chapter about the River Cats. I eagerly accepted, and was speechless during the drive home. Aside from the thrill of landing a dream job right out of college, I realized I had an enormous task ahead of me. I had to do the rich history of my city's baseball heritage justice.

After five years of research, writing and editing, I'm proud to present the finished product. This book sets out to capture the sweep of Sacramento's resplendent, albeit overlooked, baseball history that pioneered the sport in California for decades. The teams, from the highs of the pennant-winning 1942 Solons and 2007 River Cats, to the lows of the bottom-feeding 1950s Solons. The lineage of eccentric owners who led these franchises through thick and thin, like Lew Moreing and Art Savage. The fascinating in-betweens, from Gehrig and Ruth visiting town in 1927 to the Mays-McCovey San Francisco Giants playing at Edmonds Field just before its destruction in 1964. And, of course, the dozens of brilliant players and coaches who are connected to the city by birth, school or minor league upbringing. Additionally, there is space dedicated to perhaps the greatest River City baseball legend: Ron King, Sacramento's all-star MLB scout.

Even without a major league team, the River City deserves to be universally hailed as a true "baseball town," and not just by Sacramento residents and California baseball fans in general. Any fan in any region should readily think of this city when they think of America's game.

As you read each page, you will see why in great detail.

PROLOGUE

For the first half of the 20th century, Major League Baseball flourished on the East Coast and Midwest of the United States. Yankees sluggers like Babe Ruth, Lou Gehrig, Joe DiMaggio and Mickey Mantle socked volleys of home runs into the New York City sky, turning the franchise into the sports leading championship juggernaut. Connie Mack's Philadelphia Athletics excelled with regal pitching from Lefty Grove and muscular hitting by Jimmie Foxx. Ty Cobb tore up the base paths in Detroit for the Tigers. The Gashouse Gang and Stan Musial brought as much character as they did championship prestige to the St. Louis Cardinals in the '30s and '40s respectively.

During this period, the West Coast was strangely bereft of major league play. Most notably, the state of California, despite its clement weather, diverse population and abundance of major cities, lacked a team. On May 28, 1957, however, that would all change when National League owners voted unanimously to allow the New York Giants and Brooklyn Dodgers to move to the Golden State at the midseason owners meeting in Chicago. After finishing the remainder of the 1957 season in New York, the Giants transplanted to San Francisco, while the Dodgers took up residence south in Los Angeles.

When both teams commenced play in California the next year, baseball truly lived up to its adage as the national pastime. A veritable manifest destiny, the Dodgers' and Giants' respective moves to Los Angeles and San Francisco represented the sport's geographical and economic fulfillment. Not long after, the expansion Los Angeles Angels (known through many other iterations now as the Los Angeles Angels of Anaheim) took the field in 1961. This span would be bookended by the arrival of the Athletics in Oakland from Kansas City in 1968, and finally the expansion San Diego Padres in 1969.

In the more than half-century of Major League Baseball in California, these five teams have given the Golden State an unparalleled pedigree in America's game. As of this writing, they've combined for 26 pennants and 13 World Series titles. Among the legendary players to take the field under the warm California sun are: Willie Mays, Willie McCovey, Sandy Koufax, Don Drysdale, Reggie Jackson, Tony Gwynn, Vida Blue, Rollie Fingers, Steve Garvey, Maury Wills, Ozzie Smith, Fernando Valenzuela, Joe Rudi, Mark McGwire, Barry Bonds, Madison Bumgarner, Jeff Kent, Barry Zito, Mike Trout, Jim Edmonds, Manny Machado, Orlando Cepeda, Trevor Hoffman, Rod Carew, Orel Hershiser, Tim Hudson, Gaylord Perry, Catfish Hunter, Clayton Kershaw, Juan Marichal, Albert Pujols, Mike Piazza, Nolan Ryan, Dennis Eckersley, and Buster Posey.

Even without accounting for school and minor league teams, these players and franchises alone make California, as author Mark Tennis put it, "The Baseball Capital of the World." Yet to focus solely on the exploits of MLB franchises would be to neglect the teams and players that made the game thrive in the state well before them. Starting in the late 19th century, professional teams from San Francisco, Oakland, San Diego, Los Angeles and other cities flourished. Some even provided springboards for major league legends, with the Pacific Coast League's San Francisco Seals and San Diego Padres respectively cultivating the immortal talents of Joe DiMaggio and Ted Williams.

When we move our attention to the state's central valley, we find especially overlooked but resplendent history in the capital city of Sacramento. Despite never having served as home for the multitude of MLB teams to reside in California, the River City has been the hometown and training ground for many players and coaches, including All-Stars, winning managers, World Series heroes, and no-hitter and perfect game pitchers. For decades, the beloved Edmonds Field hosted the Sacramento Senators and Solons of the Pacific Coast League. Most recently, the land by the Tower Bridge along the Sacramento River has been home to the River Cats, arguably the finest minor league franchise in the country, since 2000.

All told, the saga of Sacramento baseball has always been at the forefront of the sport's development in California. It is a quintessential baseball tale; one that begins with the game's storied origins in the mid-19th century, and weaves together hometown stars, thrilling pennant chases, lean years of losing, fan loyalty, heartbreak, and redemptive triumph.

ONE

FIRST OFFICIAL BASEBALL GAME IN CALIFORNIA AND SACRAMENTO'S EARLY TEAMS

In the mid-to-late 19th century, the newfound game of baseball rapidly evolved from a novel amateur sport to a professional endeavor that spanned nationwide. After the first official game took place in Hoboken, New Jersey in June 1846, baseball surged in popularity for the next several decades as amateur teams proliferated, and the official rules of the game were codified. By the late 1860s and early '70s, the idea of paid players (as well as the best ones forming teams) had grown to the point where baseball could no longer remain a purely amateur pursuit, with the National Association becoming the first professional league in 1871.

Derived from the English sports of cricket and rounders, the exact point at which baseball was created earlier in the century remains a subject of mystery to this day. Fortunately, the historical record is less ambiguous in showing how deeply Sacramento is woven into the thread of the game's rapid evolution. The first written record of baseball in the city was in the *Daily Union* in November 1859, which described a local base ball club (the sport's name was written as two separate words back then) that had organized under

"New York rules." These local players pioneered the game in Sacramento just before it would grow in tandem with seismic shifts in U.S. history.

The year was 1860, a full decade after California was officially established as a U.S. state. In April, a solitary horse and rider galloped 1,700 miles from Sacramento to St. Joseph, Missouri with a sack of mail, establishing the U.S. Pony Express. In December, construction workers broke ground for the state capitol building in Sacramento, but its completion would be delayed over a decade by a tumultuous change in national politics California helped set in motion the month prior. On November 6, California voters narrowly voted for Republican nominee Abraham Lincoln over his Democratic and Southern Democratic rivals in the U.S. presidential election, helping him win the White House. 11 southern U.S. states seceded in protest, setting the stage for the Civil War's commencement in April 1861.

At the outset of a year that saw California and its capital city involved in transformative national events, it was none other than Sacramento that played home to the first complete game of baseball in the state's history. It took place on February 22, at the baseball tournament of the California State Fair. In this contest, the San Francisco Eagles defeated the Sacramento Club and were awarded a "Silver Ball" trophy.

Nine years later, in September 1869, the Cincinnati Red Stockings (generally recognized by historians as the first openly professional baseball team in the United States) came to town for a game with a ragtag group of local players. It was a match-up made possible by more history, that of the transcontinental railroad's completion in May of that year. The final score: Cincinnati 50, Sacramento 6. So lopsided was the game that it didn't even go the full nine innings of regulation, instead being called after only seven.

In 1886, the River City's baseball reach would expand beyond the results of exhibition games. By this time, amateur ball clubs had largely given way to teams and leagues comprising paid professional players. The California League, the first professional league in the state, was officially founded in 1883. Initially only featuring several clubs in San Francisco, it expanded to include the Sacramento Altas, the best local team in the city, in '86. Blessed with a home field dubbed Agricultural Park, located between H and 20th and E and 23rd Streets, fans flocked to see the Altas for 25 cents a pop, with women admitted for free.

*H and 20**th Streets in the present day. Photos taken by Morgan Garvey.*

The corner of H and 23rd Streets today. Photos taken by Morgan Garvey.

The corner of E and 23 Streets today. Photos taken by Morgan Garvey.

The present-day corner of E and 20th Streets. Photos taken by Morgan Garvey.

After losing their debut game 4-3 to the San Francisco Pioneers, the Altas managed to finish the 1886 season in second place with a 17-14 record. While subpar in the pitching department, their offense was superb, sporting five batters that ranked top 10 in the league. The team's name was taken from a famous northern California racehorse, apropos as Agricultural Park was adjacent to a horse racing track.

With a strong record and talented roster, the Altas earned another invitation to play in the California League in 1887. While their final record of 19-19 and third place was respectable, their pennant hopes suffered due to anemic hitting. After having a potent offense in 1886, the Altas' bats were mostly meager in '87, with only Billy Newbert's .270 average ranking among the top ten in the league. On the contrary, their pitching saw a marked improvement, thanks primarily to the redemptive season of the formerly banished Jimmy Mullee (who had been expelled by the league the previous year for likely throwing a game while pitching for the San Francisco Stars).

1888, however, would yield even less for Sacramento fans to cheer for. Team owner Wilbur George and city officials had grown frustrated with the California League, demanding more home games for the Altas and a larger percentage of gate receipts. When league officials refused, Sacramento left to play in another league altogether, which proved to be an unsuccessful move. The Altas would rejoin the California League the following year, this time with a new stadium dubbed Snowflake Park located between 28th and 30th Streets from R to S Streets. While the first game there witnessed a thrilling 11-inning victory over Oakland, the Altas couldn't sustain the winning, finishing dead last with a 33-59 record.

The 1890s witnessed greater heights for the team, albeit short-lived. Rechristened the Sacramento Senators, they amassed a 79-58 record in 1890, earning a first-place tie with San Francisco. Four of their hitters ranked in the league top ten, while pitcher George Harper logged a staggering 41-26 record. 1891 saw the team post a less stirring mark of 75-73, and the California League had the franchise moved 50 miles south to Stockton. They failed to improve in the Port City, and with the team mired in last place by the middle of the 1893 season, owner John J. Moore moved them back to Sacramento on July 5.

The change of scenery didn't yield better results, and on August 9 the season would come to a premature end. Moore refused to put his players on the train for a long trip to Los Angeles against the Angels unless they were guaranteed $100 above expenses. Angels management wouldn't budge, and on August 14 both teams disbanded. From 1894 to 1897, the California League ceased operations, depriving Sacramento of professional baseball for four years.

Fortunately, the league re-emerged with an eight-team lineup in 1898. Sacramento's club, now owned by eccentric local entrepreneur Edward Kripp, took on the moniker of the Gilt Edge. The name came from a popular local beer made by the Ruhstaller Brewery, hardly unconventional as breweries often sponsored local teams during this era. They took to the grass at a new field in Oak Park, located on 5th Avenue between 33rd and 37th Streets.

The location of the Oak Park stadium in McClatchy Park today, fittingly replaced by another baseball field. The proportion of home field today is similar to the one the Gilt Edge played with. The house in the last photo can be seen in photos of the old Oak Park as well. Photos taken by Morgan Garvey.

The Gilt Edge proceeded to dominate the league for three consecutive seasons, finishing first each year and fielding an armada of superb players. Pitcher Charles "Demon" Doyle won 57 total games during this three-year span, with his 28 in 1899 leading the league. Another pitcher, James J. Hughes, had excelled with Baltimore and Brooklyn of the National League before going 23-9 with the Gilt Edge in 1900. Shortstop Charles "Truck" Eagan led the league with 32 extra base hits the same year.

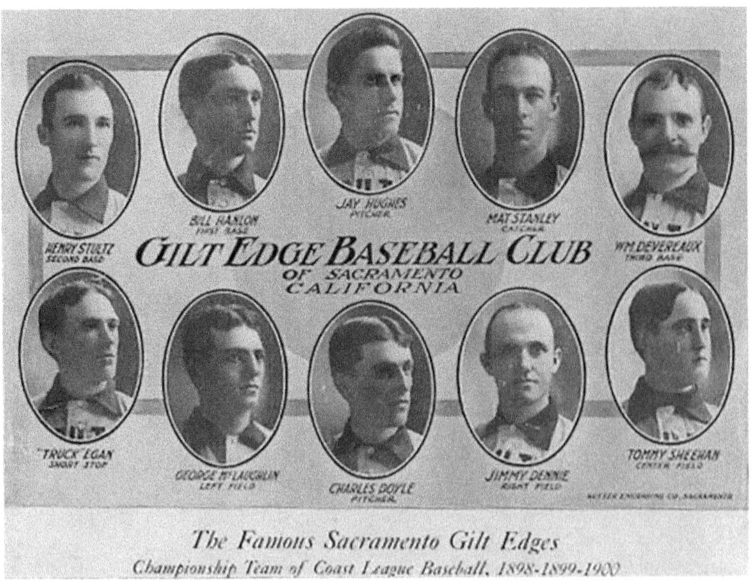

The three-time champion Gilt Edge, the first championship squads in Sacramento professional baseball history. Photo courtesy of Alan O'Connor.

Sacramento's dominance wouldn't go unchallenged for long, however, as the other California teams proceeded to upgrade their lineups. The team (re-dubbed the Senators) slipped into third place in 1901, and then dead last in 1902. But while their on-field fortunes weren't as good in 1901 and 1902, their financial fortunes improved thanks to increased fan interest and attendance. The teams in San Francisco, Oakland and Los Angeles experienced commensurate surges in gate revenue, setting the stage for a dramatic change in California baseball. Just like in the 1860s, Sacramento would be right at the forefront.

TWO

THE BIRTH AND EARLY YEARS OF THE SENATORS AND THE PACIFIC COAST LEAGUE

1900 marked the beginning of what would be dubbed "The Great American Century." After Henry Ford introduced his first gasoline engine car in 1892, the Ford Motor Company was established in 1903, ushering in the era of cars as a primary mode of transportation. The proliferation of the automobile was augmented by the seemingly boundless supply of oil, with drilling fields in many states and John D. Rockefeller's Standard Oil Trust possessing a near monopoly on national refineries.

The country was equally dominant in steel production, leading the world with 10,000,000 tons a year. Upon the assassination of President William McKinley in September 1901, Teddy Roosevelt became the youngest leader in the nation's history, and pursued a bold progressive agenda of trust-busting, natural conservation and other policies. A new form of entertainment, the motion picture, began to emerge. The sky was the limit for the United States, quite literally, when the Wright Brothers managed their first successful aircraft flights in December 1903.

The dawn of the 20th century witnessed a similarly revolutionary time in baseball. In 1901, the American League (AL) was founded and officially recognized as a major league, ending the National League's (NL) de facto monopoly over the major leagues of professional baseball. The competition between the two leagues led to exponentially greater attendance and interest in the sport.

In 1903, the AL's Boston Americans (now the Red Sox) and the NL's Pittsburgh Pirates met in the inaugural World Series, which soon became one of the most prestigious championship contests in sports and has been played every year since (minus cancellations in 1904 and 1994). In a few short years, the modern game was forged, along with the basic structure of Major League Baseball that still holds well over a century later.

In the world of California baseball, historic changes were also afoot during this period. California League owners, who had considered expanding to include teams outside the state for over a decade, finally took action in 1903 to make it a reality. Things were set in motion by San Francisco team owner Henry Harris, who pushed to incorporate Portland and Seattle into the league. There was one major impediment: this area was under the jurisdiction of the Pacific Northwest League, who had territorial rights as per the National Agreement of professional baseball.

Unfazed, Harris and his colleagues from Oakland, Los Angeles and Sacramento forged right ahead to create an "outlaw" circuit dubbed the Pacific Coast League. Stretching from Los Angeles all the way to the Canadian border, it touted a massive schedule of more than 200 games per team, which would go from March until November. For comparison, the current MLB regular season is 162 games, and runs from late March/early April until October. There would be no salary limits for players, as part of their hopes of competing directly with east coast leagues for top minor leaguers.

The Sacramento Senators made the jump from the California League to PCL play in 1903, receiving the honor of hosting the league's inaugural game on March 26. The occasion was met with festive celebration, as players from Sacramento and the visiting Oakland squad rode downtown in an automobile parade from the State House Hotel at 10th and K Streets to the Senators' stadium in Oak Park. Unfortunately, one of the cars sputtered out, forcing its occupants to make the rest of the trip in a hay wagon.

Once at the stadium, a band led the procession through the north gate, marching to second base and then to home plate. Governor George Pardee capped off the festivities by greeting all of the players and team executives before throwing out the ceremonial first pitch. Many Sacramento businesses closed at 2 P.M. to ensure fans could attend.

The Sacramento and Oakland teams ride in a motor parade to the first ever PCL game in Oak Park. Photo courtesy of Alan O'Connor.

The Senators made sure to coronate the day properly, rallying from a 4-2 deficit in the eighth inning to pull off a 7-4 comeback win over Oakland. Sacramento would go on to win the series against Oakland and then best Portland five times to open the season with a 9-4 record. However, the Los Angeles Angels started their season with 15 straight wins, setting a pace for a total of 133 that the Senators would never be able to catch. At season's end, Sacramento's second place 105-105 mark put them a whopping 27.5 games behind Los Angeles.

Even though they wouldn't win the PCL pennant, the 1903 season didn't lack highlights for the Senators. Fan attendance at Oak Park was so ample in the early part of the season that manager Mike Fisher had new bleachers installed to accommodate overflow crowds. As a team, they ranked second only to Seattle in cumulative batting average, amassing a .268 mark. They were outstanding defensively, with their team fielding average of .940 ranking only behind Los Angeles. The Senators were also torrid baserunners, swiping a league-leading 403 stolen bases.

Ultimately, Sacramento's inability to catch the Angels would affect the team's fate. The once burgeoning attendance dwindled by midseason as the team skidded around second and third place, much to Fisher's dismay. In a piece in *The Sacramento Bee*, he clearly stated he could sign better players if fans simply bought more tickets to their home games. If they didn't, he warned, the team would move north to Tacoma or Spokane in Washington.

Fisher wasn't bluffing. Upon season's end, he promptly boarded a train to Tacoma to meet with community leaders. All the same, he did make an offer to Sacramento, proposing the city Chamber of Commerce buy the club for $5,000. However, the chamber's public affairs committee stated the city had nothing to gain by buying the Senators. By year's end, they were officially moved to Tacoma, depriving Sacramento of a PCL club for the next few years. During this time, the PCL was cleared of its outlaw status by National Association President Patrick T. Powers and was officially recognized as a professional league.

Fortunately, a new outlaw league would help fill the void somewhat during this time. The California State League, which also commenced operations in 1903, added Sacramento in 1904 to a lineup of clubs from San Francisco, San Jose, Stockton, Lodi, Oakland, and San Francisco. The new Sacramento club failed to win on the field, leading to their disbanding in August. However, they would return in 1906, in time for the CSL's schedule expansion. Originally playing only on Sundays, CSL clubs began playing several times a week starting in 1907, which enabled them to coax top players away from the major leagues and the PCL.

The 1908 team (called the Senators), while finishing in third place, boasted players of former and future major league renown. First baseman Joe "Flash" Nealon played in the same infield as the legendary Hall of Fame shortstop Honus Wagner for the Pittsburgh Pirates in '06 and '07. The outfield was anchored by Harry Hooper, who would later help the Boston Red Sox win four World Series the next decade as part of a Hall of Fame career.

In 1909, Pacific Coast League baseball returned to the River City, albeit after much legal wrangling. After PCL president J. Cal Ewing proposed bringing a new team to the capital city, *The Sacramento Bee* opined that the California State League had delivered a comparable level of professional baseball, and thus the PCL wasn't necessary. Ewing still persisted in trying to convince California's outlaw clubs to join Organized Baseball and abide by its strict rules on drafting, salary caps, and reigning in players jumping their contracts for other teams. But the CSL refused, with Sacramento player-owner Charlie Graham refusing to meet their demands. He bluntly stated, "I would sooner throw up the whole thing and retire from baseball than go into Organized Baseball under any such conditions."

It would take the intervention of Major League Baseball itself to settle the dispute once and for all. American League president Ban Johnson and National League president Harry Pulliam convened with PCL and CSL officials in San Francisco just before Christmas of 1908. The meeting produced no agreement, but that didn't keep Johnson from promising to fight the CSL relentlessly unless they relinquished their outlaw status. The threat was effective, as Graham quickly changed his mind mere days later and agreed to enter his team into the Pacific Coast League. It proved a wise move, as the California State League gave up its outlaw status and joined Organized Baseball in late 1909.

Nonetheless, the 1909 Sacramento Senators remained mostly familiar to their fans. Many of the players were holdovers from the CSL team, including Graham, pitchers Fred Brown and Jimmy "The Whale" Whalen, and infielders Fred Raymer and Heinie Jansing. Their most notable acquisition for the season was an outlaw Fresno first baseman named Arnold "Chick" Gandil, who would lead the team in almost all batting categories in 1909. But it was his actions 10 years later rather than his playing that cemented his name in baseball lore, as one of eight Chicago White Sox banned from baseball for life for throwing the 1919 World Series.

The Senators would play at the old Oak Park diamond, commencing the season at home with a 6-2 victory over a new PCL team from Vernon (a suburb of Los Angeles). Yet the occasion was marred somewhat by the shoddy conditions the park had fallen into. The grandstand roof was in dire need of re-shingling, a new entrance was needed, and visiting teams didn't have a proper clubhouse.

The field itself wasn't even in proper playing condition, the grass choked with weeds and a trash pile unceremoniously dumped in front of the right field fence. The fans didn't seem to mind much, however, coming through the gates in even greater numbers than in years past. So much so that the two turnstiles at the stadium couldn't handle the influx of attendees, requiring two more to be installed.

Like the inaugural Sacramento PCL clubs, the bountiful fan attendance wasn't rewarded with a pennant. The team scuffled to a 97-107 mark, good enough for fourth place. A weak offense was their Achilles heel, suffering many shutout losses during the summer. Their pitching staff was substantially better, with two pitchers (Whalen and former outlaw Charles "Spider" Baum) winning more than 20 games.

Less fortunate in the pitching department was Jack Fitzgerald, who not only lost 25 games but made unsavory headlines away from the diamond. Toward season's end, Fitzgerald was at a K Street saloon at 3 A.M. when he got into a physical altercation with a Sacramento police detective, to the point where the officer pulled his pistol on the pitcher.

While the team's roster experienced little turnover in the offseason, their ownership lineup welcomed a high-profile addition. Charlie Graham and the rest of the shareholders were faced with a $5,000 deficit and needed an outside source to help alleviate their financial troubles.

In stepped John I. Taylor, the son of a Boston newspaper magnate and owner of the American League's Boston Red Sox. Despite being all the way across the country, Graham and Taylor were no strangers to each other. Graham's only year in the major leagues was with Boston in 1906, while Taylor obtained Harry Hooper from Graham's 1908 outlaw team.

Taylor had a reputation as a debonair bon vivant, already being familiar with the West Coast thanks to his marriage to San Francisco socialite Dorothy Van Ness. He was also just as much a savvy promoter, being responsible for one of baseball's most cherished monikers when he shortened the Red Stockings' name to the rustic and unique Red Sox. He was just the kind of dynamic, resourceful figure the club needed, and Graham courted him to become its majority owner. Taylor obliged, buying 12,000 shares (almost half of all shares) and wiping out their debt.

The move generated an ecstatic buzz in the Sacramento sports press, with the *Sacramento Union* believing it would likely "place the local club on a par with many Eastern clubs and high above the standard of a majority of the [Pacific] Coast league teams." Taylor was equally jubilant about having an ideal place for his Boston players and prospects to practice and stay in shape. He had considered many cities, but when Sacramento was recommended to him for its climate and top-notch baseball facilities for sustained training, he immediately reached out to his old friend Graham.

Upon hearing the offer, Graham was enthused, and insisted Taylor make the purchase immediately. The Boston owner was instantly sold, save for one concern: attendance. Graham responded by conceding that the team's current stadium was the cause for meager patronage, and that they were close to securing a new park that would solve the problem. Taylor was persuaded, and thus became majority owner.

With finances set in order, Taylor wasted no time overhauling the team's staid roster. Power-hitting first baseman Harold "Babe" Danzig was brought over from the New England League, along with pitcher Ben Hunt, outfielders William "Hank" Perry and Hap Briggs, and third baseman Louis Boardman. The latter two were especially promising young players, having hit close to .290 the season prior. Graham gave the outfield a boost by signing Edward "Deacon" Van Buren from the CSL, who would patrol the grass for Sacramento for the next five years.

An even bigger change for the club was the advent of a new stadium. Edward Kripp, former owner of the champion Gilt Edge of the 1890s, had a new facility built at 11th and Y Streets (Riverside Boulevard and Broadway today). Bearing the name Buffalo Park (also named after a local brewery), it was Sacramento's finest stadium yet, featuring spacious bleachers and a towering wooden grandstand that gave fans "a perfect, unobstructed view" according to the *Sacramento Union*. It was christened by an exhibition game against none other than Chick Gandil and the White Sox, who won 8-3.

Baseball action at Buffalo Park in its inaugural year of 1910. While it would undergo various name changes and reconstructions, this location would remain the home of the Sacramento PCL club until 1960. Photo courtesy of Alan O'Connor.

On paper, the 1910 Sacramento Senators should have been a vast improvement over the 1909 incarnation. They had a state-of-the-art ballpark near the city, an improved financial situation, a revamped team, and an enthusiastic new owner intent on winning. Pundits from other cities believed the Senators were a sure pick to win the PCL. The sports gossip column of the *Union* was especially optimistic, opining that "instead of hanging their heads in doubt this season Sacramento fans may wave the colors high and hail the victors that can even now be seen upon the horizon bearing home the banners of the enemy."

The first regular season game at Buffalo would seem to be a harbinger of that, when the Senators blasted their way to an 18-2 victory. Yet 1910 would prove to be far worse than the previous year as one misfortune piled on to another. After the opening day blowout, the Senators were in last place immediately thereafter. Numerous players succumbed to injury, the most brutal coming when infielder Fred Raymer was knocked unconscious by a beanball for four hours.

The pitching staff, aside from being woeful statistically, made headlines for embarrassing behavior. Jimmy Whalen was fined $25 and suspended for punching an umpire; Jack Fitzgerald, already notorious for his row with the police the year before, was suspended for failing to show up for a game in San Francisco. The offense was downright feeble, amassing two scoreless streaks of 38 and 40 innings late in the season. When Los Angeles closed the door on Sacramento's listless year with a 4-0 shutout, the Senators finished dead last in the PCL at 83-128.

Once again, Taylor reshaped the team in hopes of yielding better results in 1911. Graham retired from playing to work exclusively as an executive, handing over the on-field managerial reins to new infielder James "Patsy" O'Rourke. The hard-nosed newcomer quickly implemented a new culture of discipline for the players. They were now required to be in bed by midnight, out of bed by 8 A.M., and present at Buffalo Park for daily training no later than 10 A.M. sharp. No player could leave the grounds without his permission and were to avoid heavy drinking before games. The last rule was certainly most applicable to Jack Fitzgerald, whose alcoholism had derailed his potential and fueled reckless behavior in recent years.

A new lineup and O'Rourke's rigorous discipline made little difference in 1911. The Senators amassed a 95-109 record, not bad enough for last place but only placing them fourth out of six. Sacramento's pitching staff provided the lion's share of highlights, chiefly Spider Baum. The right-hander pitched a 19-inning victory over Portland, one of eight victories he racked up during July and August. O'Rourke's regimen managed to whip Fitzgerald into shape, yielding a 20-17 record. The man who was once suspended for failing to show made an especially historic start on September 11, when he pitched all 24 innings of a game that tied for the longest in PCL history.

Ironically, it was O'Rourke himself who showed the greatest lack of discipline on the field. In a July home game that was played in Stockton, O'Rourke's temper got the better of him as he unloaded a punch on umpire George Hildebrand, leading to a two-week suspension. O'Rourke's antics weren't what did the team in, but rather its weak offense and fielding. Granted, they weren't as bad as a typo in the *Reach* baseball guide that had the offense collectively going 0-for-7,104.

In spite of his on-field spat in Stockton, O'Rourke came back to manage the following season. He intensified his stringent training routine, moving spring training 40 miles north in the quieter town of Marysville to ensure no distractions. The biggest change wasn't on the field, but in the ownership. In a stunning move that wasn't disclosed until June, Spokane, WA bookmaker Jack Atkin bought half of the team's 25,000 shares, including all of John I. Taylor's stock. When news of the purchase finally broke in June, O'Rourke stepped down as manager and let veteran outfielder Deacon Van Buren take over the position.

Despite all this, 1912 was a leap backwards for the Senators. Sacramento tumbled further in the standings to dead last, winning only 73 games against 121 losses. Mounting injuries and O'Rourke's "revolving door" approach to assembling the roster were the main culprits, although Van Buren did manage a .313 average even while taking on managerial duties.

For 1913, Jack Atkin and Charlie Graham felt the answer to their troubles lay in hiring a former major leaguer as manager. Germany Schaeffer, an infielder who played alongside Ty Cobb for the World Series Detroit Tigers the prior decade, was a strong consideration. Another was Doc White, the stalwart pitcher for the 1906 "Hitless Wonders" Chicago White Sox that won the World Series against the heavily favored Chicago Cubs. Coincidentally, another candidate was White's '06 teammate Billy Sullivan, who literally went hitless in that series.

The job ultimately went to Harry Wolverton, a former player who had both PCL and MLB managerial credentials. In the former capacity, he steered the Oakland Oaks to respectable finishes in 1910 and 1911. But he wasn't at the helm for their 1912 PCL pennant-winning season, as he was in the majors leading the New York Highlanders (later the Yankees).

As was the case the past few years, Wolverton felt a roster shake-up and a strict routine for players would yield better results on the field. There were only 10 returnees, including Patsy O'Rourke and Deacon Van Buren, and nine new players. Whether new or returning, however, all players were equally subject to an austere set of rules. Drinking after sunset, playing cards and shooting dice were outlawed, and Wolverton had harsh punishments to ensure those vices were held in check. A first violation would lead to a $25 fine, with a second leading to outright expulsion from the team.

Wolverton's no-nonsense approach yielded results. After winning just 73 games the previous season, Sacramento won 103 in 1913. It wasn't enough to catch first-place Portland, but in addition to a second-place finish, it generated new levels of fan interest. By midseason, the crowds were so enormous that an additional bleacher section was built at Buffalo Park to accommodate them.

After such a successful turnaround, Sacramento seemed to be on the doorstep of a pennant in 1914. The team had come within striking distance in 1913, and fans were coming to Buffalo Park in waves like never before. The new ownership refurbished the stadium accordingly, adding fresh new grass, sprinklers to maintain it, and a parking lot to accommodate fans who came by automobile (now a mainstream source of transportation). Wolverton had the left field wall moved in 50 feet, creating more space for cars to park behind it.

Buffalo Park's renovation wasn't the only development that heightened expectations for 1914. Wolverton reached an agreement with the Detroit Tigers that stipulated Detroit would provide prime talent for Sacramento throughout the season, in exchange for selecting any Senators player of their choice at season's end. Additionally, he now split ownership duties with Lloyd Jacobs, a San Francisco insurance broker who helped him acquire 18,000 shares of the team's stock. The club even sported new uniforms, white with a black pinstripe at home and gray with blue and white stripes on the road.

The anticipation for the new-look Senators and their revamped ballpark was consummated on opening day when Governor Hiram Johnson threw the first pitch, a curve that landed over the plate for a strike. For all intents and purposes, it was the best pitch Sacramento would muster all day. Portland trounced the Senators 8-1, a harbinger of things to come as the team was maddeningly inconsistent all season long. They vacillated between brief winning and extended losing streaks so much that *The Sacramento Bee* ran the following poem after one six-game skid:

> *"O, golly gee, I hate to see*
> *The scoreboards nowadays;*
> *For it does seem our Solon team*
> *Has fallen on evil ways;*
> *It lost its grip on the southern trip*
> *Each man played like a chump;*
> *At a speedy clip, it began to dip*
> *To the bottom of the dump."*

Wolverton was criticized for his reliance on veterans over younger players, and constantly signed and released players. One notable name that came through this revolving door was pitcher Claude "Lefty" Williams, who along with ex-Sacramento player Chick Gandil would later be banned from baseball for throwing the 1919 World Series with the White Sox. Even veteran Babe Danzig returned to play first base, but he was a shadow of the star he was in 1910 and 1911.

By August, the team was drifting in fifth place when rumors began to circulate that they would soon be moving to Seattle. Wolverton flatly denied them, but on the last day of the month, he and Lloyd Jacobs met with PCL directors in Oakland to discuss moving the team to San Francisco. Decreasing fan interest was cited as the primary factor, and the team had a chance to entertain far more fans in the Bay Area. They would play some home games in Oakland when the Oaks were away and the rest in San Francisco when the Seals were on the road. Oakland alone had a population of 200,000, 140,000 more than Sacramento.

The Senators now became the San Francisco Missions, but the Sacramento press was incensed by their sudden departure. The *Bee* took issue with the ownership's logic that weak fan attendance necessitated the move, given the team's declining quality in play was commensurate with the drop in fans filling the stands. Simply put, if they played better, attendance would improve.

The *Union* considered it an insult to the entire city, particularly because Wolverton and Jacobs made no effort to contact potential financial backers who could have kept the team in Sacramento. In any event, switching to Oakland and San Francisco did the team no favors, as they finished the season second to last place.

The same month the Senators made their unceremonious move to the Bay Area, Russia and Germany declared war on each other four days after Austria-Hungary declared war on Serbia. It was the beginning of World War I, which would become the deadliest conflict in human history, claiming over 20 million lives and reshaping the course of the 20th century. The sinking of the *Lusitania* the following year galvanized sentiment for the U.S. to finally enter the war. For the next three years, Sacramento was without a baseball team.

During the intervening years from 1914 to 1917, U.S. President Woodrow Wilson was steadfast in keeping the nation out of the conflict. But in 1917, he reversed course and officially entered the war, a decision that impacted Sacramento directly. 4,000 fighting-age men enlisted right away, while Globe Iron Works won a government contract to build military aircraft in the city. Mather Air Force Base was established to provide flight training for pilots. Many women took up railroad and iron works jobs that had been vacated by men who enlisted.

One American industry that certainly wasn't bolstered by the war effort was baseball. The sport's popularity had already taken a hit from new forms of entertainment like movies and pool gambling, and falling attendance caused many professional leagues to fold entirely. The Pacific Coast League managed to weather the storm, but nonetheless suffered a steep decline in attendance. In November of 1917, three PCL owners refused to play in the upcoming season unless the league's financially unsustainable Portland club was moved or replaced by a more conveniently located team.

This set of circumstances opened up a chance for baseball to return to Sacramento after three years. Charlie Graham and clothier Charles J. Heeseman stepped in and purchased the Portland franchise, moving it to the River City and naming them the Senators like the previous team. While they sported brand new uniforms (now with a blue "S" emblazoned on a red heart), the team's roster was hardly as pristine, mostly made up of aging veterans juxtaposed with unproven young players.

The Senators flitted between first, third and fifth place before a dire announcement from U.S. Provost Marshal Enoch Crowder in May changed the course of the season. Crowder implemented a "work or fight" amendment to the original regulations regarding the enlistment of men in the armed forces. It stipulated that any men in "idle" positions immaterial to the war effort were thus required to take up a job that aided it, or otherwise enlist and fight.

Unsurprisingly, playing baseball was labeled a nonessential line of work under this order, and the entire sport felt the effects of it right away. Hundreds of major league stars went off to Europe, among them future Hall of Famers Christy Mathewson, Ty Cobb, Grover Alexander, Herb Pennock, Sam Rice, Branch Rickey, Burleigh Grimes, and Waite Hoyt. Some players lost their lives to the cause, with Eddie Grant and Bun Troy both killed in action in France.

The Senators in particular lost many key players to the war effort, with catcher Gus Fisher moving to Portland to work at a shipyard and outfielder Dennis Wilie and several others working at a sugar refinery in Crockett, CA. Additionally, a "war tax" had been imposed on tickets, bumping the cost of bleacher seats from 25 cents to 28 and grandstand seats from 50 cents to 55. As a result of the extra shifts necessary for war manufacturing, fans weren't able to attend games as much, leading to a dip in attendance.

Ultimately, these conditions proved too much for the PCL to overcome, ending the season abruptly on July 14 a full three months before its usual finish date. The league was lucky to even survive at all, as two other leagues, the American Association and the International League, folded entirely in 1918. The Senators' record was frozen at 48-48, fourth place behind Vernon, Los Angeles and San Francisco.

Fortunately, World War I finally came to an end on November 11 of that year. 1919 looked to be a much smoother year for the Senators and baseball as a whole. The Pacific Coast League expanded to eight teams, incorporating franchises in Seattle and Portland. The Senators made some acquisitions to upgrade their pitching staff, the most notable being future Hall of Famer Charles "Dazzy" Vance. The staff also sported local darling Walter Mails, a former *Sacramento Bee* paperboy who attended Christian Brothers High School.

The 1919 team proved to be basically the same as the truncated 1918 campaign. Like many Sacramento teams, they were strong in fielding, base-running and pitching, but weak at the plate. Despite never being much of a threat to frontrunners Vernon and Los Angeles, fans turned out in droves. So much, in fact, that the total attendance for the season ended up exceeding Sacramento's own population of 65,000. The team even earned a new nickname, the Solons, which kept appearing in headlines during a winning spell in July. However, it wouldn't become their official name until much later.

But even a nine-game winning streak couldn't salve a fast-growing rift between manager Bill Rodgers and third baseman Babe Pinelli. Pinelli had already been sold to play for the New York Yankees the next year in 1920, and thus chose to take his time showing up to Buffalo Park one day while healing from a foot injury. An incensed Rodgers had the third baseman's pay cut by $25, leading an enraged Pinelli to challenge his skipper to a brawl in the clubhouse.

Rodgers obliged, and the two had a closed-door scrap to vent their frustrations with each other. Pinelli was getting the better of his boss when several other players broke down the clubhouse door to break up the fight. While there were no hard feelings between the two afterward, it did nothing to affect the team for better or worse, which finished in fourth place at 85-83.

Yet the greatest headlines for the team didn't come from on-field play or a clubhouse scrap, but rather ownership changes. At season's end, Sacramento director Lewis Moreing made his pitch to buy the team, which was looking at some $10,000 in losses and $14,000 in debt despite record-setting attendance in 1919. Moreing and his brother Charles assumed the debt, and Lew became the sole owner on December 5.

It was an unprecedented change for the franchise. After years of joint ownership by various shareholders, the team was now in the hands of a single magnate who throatily promised nothing short of greatness. "I am going to endeavor to give Sacramento a pennant-winning team," declared Moreing. "With a team that is up in the race, I believe there is not a better city in the country than Sacramento and the fans will have a team next season that will give them all a battle if such an achievement is possible." He would own the club for 13 years, and Sacramento baseball would be revolutionized in multiple regards.

THREE

1920-1933: THE LEW MOREING ERA

Lew Moreing was just the kind of owner every fan wants, and every team needs. That is, an ambitious one with deep pockets and a limitless desire to do anything to help the team succeed. Going into 1920, things were looking a lot like a decade before in 1910, when the entrepreneurial John I. Taylor became majority owner and the team moved into brand new Buffalo Park.

Unlike in 1910, there wouldn't be a new stadium, but Moreing nonetheless made massive adjustments to the team's current home. Buffalo Park's bleachers were moved from right field to left field, and a new grandstand was added by the first base line that expanded the seating capacity to 6,000. Like previous new owners and managers, he wasted no time fine-tuning the

A photo of Lew Moreing taken in 1928. His enormous personal wealth and even bigger ambitions redefined Sacramento baseball in many ways. Photo courtesy of Alan O'Connor.

roster to create a winner. Dazzy Vance was traded to Memphis for cash, as was first baseman Art Griggs to the St. Louis Cardinals. Frederick "Fritz" Mollwitz was signed as Griggs' replacement for $4,000. Veterans like Walter "Duster" Mails, Hick Cady, Les Cook, and Bill Prough returned to round out the roster.

In spite of all this, Sacramento completed the mirror image of the 1910 team by failing to live up to expectations. Things started to go awry in May, when outfielder Brick Eldred was suspended and fined for insubordinate behavior towards manager Bill Rodgers. He was subsequently shipped to Seattle, a most regrettable move as he quickly blossomed into one of the best batters in the PCL. This was especially disappointing as Sacramento once again failed to perform at the plate, ranking dead last in the league in team hitting. The season ended at 89-109, second to last only ahead of Portland.

One player, however, would taste championship glory in 1920. Pitcher Walter Mails, the popular local boy, drew the attention of MLB's Cleveland Indians, who sent $10,000 and two players just to acquire him. Their investment paid off in spades, as Mails won seven games and helped the Indians win their first World Series in franchise history, even pitching a three-hit shutout in game six against Brooklyn.

He returned at October's end to a hero's welcome in Sacramento, with a mob of cheering fans surrounding the Southern Pacific station upon his arrival. After being serenaded by the Sacramento Boys' Band, he rode alongside Lew and Charles Moreing in a lengthy parade from the railroad station to City Hall. In front of some 2,500 adoring fans, Mails earnestly expressed his gratitude for the letters and telegrams they sent him as he helped Cleveland win the championship.

"I went up there with confidence, feeling that I could at least win some games, but I did not dream I would be so successful," he said in his address. "If I put Sacramento on the map, as you say I did, Cleveland is glad that it is on the map. I want to thank you all from the bottom of my heart for the reception you have given me, and to tell you that I am certainly glad to be back in Sacramento once more." Mails showed just as much recognition for his former Sacramento teammates, temporarily breaking away from the mob of fans to have a friendly chat with Bill Prough, Billy Orr, Fred Mollwitz and several others.

As for the Senators, their weak season didn't warrant a parade of any kind. Rather, it put them once again in a precarious financial situation. Moreing was frustrated by what he perceived as insufficient fan support, while the team had massive operating costs to cover. In a move hardly becoming of his bold promises to lead the franchise to success, he implored the Sacramento Chamber of Commerce to take over the team's financial operations.

When that failed, he announced his intention to find another buyer. This likely had a galvanic effect on the team, who finished the season at a torrid pace, winning 18 of 22 home games. Fans accordingly turned out in droves, and Moreing was satisfied with the ensuing profits enough to renege on his threats of selling.

However, there was grim news that drew many fans' attention away from Sacramento's ups and downs. Unlike World War I, these headlines came from the baseball world itself. The Pacific Coast League was rocked by a scandal when it was revealed that players from multiple teams intentionally threw games in 1919, allowing Vernon to win that year's pennant. The players fingered in the affair were Bill Rumler and Harl Maggert of Salt Lake City, San Francisco's Casey Smith and Tom Seaton, and Vernon's own Babe Borton. Even though

Sacramento's hero in the 1920 world's series, who arrived home yesterday and was met at the Southern Pacific depot by a crowd of enthusiastic fans, estimated at between two and three thousand. The star hurler of the Cleveland club will be guest of honor at a Chamber of Commerce banquet to be given at 6:30 o'clock Friday evening at Hotel Land.

Mails in his Senators uniform. Photo from The Sacramento Union, courtesy of the California Digital Newspaper Collection.

a Los Angeles grand jury didn't officially indict them, all five players were still banned by PCL president William H. McCarthy.

Far bigger in national headlines was the "Black Sox" Scandal in Major League Baseball, where eight Chicago White Sox players were accused of throwing the 1919 World Series, and ultimately banned for life by commissioner Kenesaw Mountain "Judge" Landis in 1921. This scandal carried significance for Sacramento baseball fans, as two of the "eight men out" were former Senators players Chick Gandil and Claude "Lefty" Williams.

Fortunately, the on-field action took center stage again in 1921. The season would witness, to date, the greatest pennant chase in PCL history, with Sacramento just one of five teams jockeying for the crown all season long. The Senators managed to contend with virtually the same team as the year before. Almost everyone in the infield led the league in fielding in their respective positions, and the pitching rotation was brilliant.

Unlike many previous years where the team fizzled out by the middle of the year (if they were even contending at all), Sacramento fought valiantly all season in 1921. At the midpoint, they were an excellent 53-39 and in third place. Their first huge test in the pennant race came in late August, when San Francisco came to Buffalo Park for a high stakes seven-game stand. The Seals led the Senators in the standings by five games, making a series victory imperative for Sacramento. However, San Francisco managed to edge them four games to three, preserving the lead they had all year long.

Even then, the Senators weren't too far behind as the season reached its finale. In a dramatic final week, Sacramento and Los Angeles were deadlocked for second place behind San Francisco at 102-78. Los Angeles proceeded to win five of its last seven games in Portland to leapfrog San Francisco for the pennant, who lost five of seven in Seattle. Sacramento, meanwhile, won three of five games in Vernon to secure a second-place finish. Altogether, it was a historically great year for the PCL, as six of its eight teams finished with winning records.

With better hitting, the Senators might have won the PCL title. Once again, fielding and pitching were their foundation. They led the league defensively with a team fielding percentage of .972, while the pitching staff was brilliant front to back. Paul Fittery led them all with a staggering 25 wins, with Bill Prough right behind him at 20. Elmer Shea (nicknamed "Specs" for his glasses) had the lowest win total of any starter, a solid 12. The rotation combined for 17 shutout victories, the most in the league.

The offense, on the other hand, didn't put up similarly superlative numbers. Their team average of .278, while respectable, ranked them second to last in the league. It might have been enough to win the pennant in previous years, but in a season of such unprecedented success for the entire PCL, it wasn't nearly enough. Even with 105 wins, Moreing wasn't satisfied with a second-place finish, and made the shocking decision to relieve Rodgers of his managerial duties. Infielder Charlie Pick was tapped as his successor.

Even bigger than the sudden change in manager was a change in venue. On November 25, 1921, workers started tearing apart Buffalo Park's antiquated wooden seating structures. They were replaced with a sturdier concrete base, topped by 10,000 seats and a towering outer wall roof that would shelter fans from the broiling summer sun. To access this new grandstand, a ramp extending from the corner of Riverside and Y Streets was added as well.

Rechristened Moreing Field, the new home of the Senators was state of the art in every facet. In addition to more seats, there was a bigger concession stand, more parking, and a new women's restroom. The players and umpires could enjoy much nicer quarters, and the locker rooms had more space, heating and better showers. The field was built for the purest form of baseball, with right field being extended from 280 feet from home plate to 330. As a result, very few home runs were hit at the park throughout the 1922 season, a stark contrast to the proliferation of homers in the majors ignited by Yankees slugger Babe Ruth during that period.

The stadium drew effusive praise before the Senators even took the field, and even before its finishing touches were implemented. In a report in February 1922, *Sacramento Union* writer Win J. Cutter marveled: "Just now the new park stands unclothed, but the huge skeleton of the marvelous structure stands forth in all its glory of a dream which resolved into achievement. It awaits now but the finishing touches of the carpenter and painter to stand forth as a monument to man's plan...to seize opportunity and to overcome obstacles. Sacramento owes much to the Moreings and the fans should show their appreciation of the strong faith which these men are reposing in the future of Sacramento."

A photo of Moreing Field during its celebrated renovation in 1922. Inset photos show, from left to right, Charles and Lew Moreing. Photo from The Sacramento Union, *courtesy of the California Digital Newspaper Archive.*

The heightened expectations made the on-field results of 1922 even more painful. Injuries depleted the lineup from the get go, including player-manager Charlie Pick. Moreing tried to patch the team's holes with unproven young players and marginal backups he could sign for cheap, which led to fewer fans attending his polished stadium. Far removed from the 105-win team that came within striking distance of a pennant, the Senators tumbled into the cellar with a meager 76 wins. In addition to a staggering 18 total injuries, every starting pitcher posted a losing record.

1923, fortunately, proved a much more successful outing for River City baseball. After years of terrible-to-mediocre offense, the bats exploded for a .298 team average, while setting team records for runs, hits, doubles, and total bases. Granted, this improvement was congruent with professional baseball as a whole, which had entered the "live ball" era of increased home run totals. But it didn't make the potency of Sacramento's offense any less impressive. Six members of the lineup hit over .300, with catcher Art Koehler's muscular .356 leading the pack.

Once again, pitching and fielding were of note. The defense led the league with a .968 team fielding percentage, and the pitching staff had two 20-game winners. The most colorful pitcher was Moses "Chief" Yellow Horse, a burly Pawnee Indian who led the staff in wins and innings pitched. Yet the Chief was as undisciplined as he was talented. In one instance in July, he stormed off the mound in a fit of anger after arguing with Pick, resulting in a then-hefty $250 fine. When an injury plagued his pitching arm, he turned to excessive liquor consumption as his remedy, which earned him a demotion to the Texas League and a hastened end to his playing career.

While the Senators didn't attain their much-sought pennant in 1923, they still amassed 112 wins, a franchise record. 1924 would also prove to be a year to remember for the Senators. That is, the Washington Senators in the major leagues, who won a thrilling World Series over the New York Giants. The Sacramento Senators, meanwhile, were the exact opposite, inexplicably tumbling into last place. After supreme hitting and fielding the previous season, Sacramento's bats and gloves suddenly had a reverse Midas Touch. What made things even more galling was that they boasted virtually the same lineup as 1923, yet didn't come anywhere near the same results.

The only player who maintained his excellence from the prior season was outfielder and local favorite Earl McNeely. But in an ironic twist, McNeely's excellent play would send him to none other than the Washington Senators. Moreing agreed to send McNeely to Calvin Griffith's club in exchange for $35,000 and three players to be named later.

Long derided for being "First in war, first in peace, and last in the American League," Washington was in the midst of a miraculous push for the American League pennant and thus a trip to the World Series. McNeely was integral to Washington's pennant run, playing alongside future Hall of Famers like Walter "Big Train" Johnson, Goose Goslin, Sam Rice, and "boy wonder" player-manager Bucky Harris. The crowning moment game in game seven of the World Series against the New York Giants, when McNeely laced the winning hit in the bottom of the 12th inning to end one of the greatest Fall Classics ever played.

The Sacramento Senators, meanwhile, enjoyed no such highlights in 1924. Their most memorable episode came in September, when trainer Jack Downey subject pitcher Seal Lion Hall to a particularly brutal beating. It wasn't the first physical altercation between members of the Senators club, but in this instance, one of the men involved was an actual fighter. Downey was a heavyweight boxer who fought a trilogy against the legendary Jack Dempsey, winning the first time but losing the next two.

All three fights took place in Salt Lake City, where the Senators had just wrapped up a series. Hall took to taunting Downey about his losses, and Downey was angered to the point of proving his fistic prowess anew. He administered a hefty beating, and upon the team's return to Sacramento, immediately admitted his mistake to Moreing. Expecting to be fired, Moreing instead gave Downey permission to slug Hall anytime he so pleased. Contrary to his expectations of being fired right then and there, he would retain his job for two more decades.

While things would work out in the long run for Downey, the Sacramento Senators' present situation was hardly desirable. They finished 88-112, dead last in the PCL standings. Despite some ambitious roster retooling by Moreing, 1925 proved to more of the same, leading to a decline in attendance. Moreing resumed his threats to sell the club as soon as possible but found no takers. The team did manage a late season surge, but it was only enough to place them at second to last rather than the familiar bottom of the standings.

Going into the 1926 season, the players hoped to cleanse themselves of their last place ways. Fittingly, they took a week in March to soak in the spa waters of Richardson Springs northeast of Chico. It worked…at least a little. The team improved to 99-102, which translated to an uninspiring fifth place finish. Sacramento fans, however, were certainly satisfied, with attendance rising by 171,000 and giving Moreing an influx of extra cash with which he could improve the club for next season.

Moreing didn't hesitate to try and build a pennant winner for 1927, trading and buying multiple players. His best move came when he shipped catcher Merv Shea to the Detroit Tigers for three players and cash considerations.

While Shea would go on to an underwhelming major league career, the Senators immediately reaped the rewards of the players they got in return. They improved to a 100-95 record and amassed a .287 team average, which would probably be good enough for first place in most seasons but strangely only got them to fourth.

The season didn't yield a pennant as hoped, but it was nonetheless an uptick for the franchise. Attendance shot even further up to 177,700, staving off any potential threats of moving by Moreing. By far the most indelible highlight, however, didn't come in the regular season, but just after its end. Moreover, it was courtesy of two hallowed legends who were far from Sacramento: New York Yankees superstars Babe Ruth and Lou Gehrig. Just days removed from a dominant World Series victory over Pittsburgh, the future Hall of Famers were "barnstorming" across the country with teams of local players.

Since Major League Baseball hadn't expanded to the West Coast yet (a process that wouldn't happen until 1958), California fans had only heard of Ruth and Gehrig through newspapers and stories, almost as if they were fabled characters. But October of 1927 witnessed the two men come to the Golden State to play exhibition games in San Francisco, Marysville, Stockton, Sacramento, and San Jose. On October 25th, the "Bustin' Babes" and "Larrupin' Lous" took to the grass at Moreing Field, with some of the Sacramento Senators playing in their lineups. Some 6,000 packed the stands as Gehrig's squad beat Ruth's by a score of 10-7.

Having seen the best players of MLB's champs play on their field, it was only fitting the Senators themselves ascended to pennant-winning heights in 1928. It was a feat that was long overdue, as the Senators had never won a title in the PCL era, and the city of Sacramento hadn't tasted a championship of any kind since the Gilt Edge claimed the California League crown in 1900.

After years of waiting, the Senators finally rewarded their fans with a regal season in 1928. They did it with basically the same roster as 1927, boosted by the notable addition of hard-hitting first baseman Earl Sheely, who came to Sacramento from the Chicago White Sox organization. Already known for being one of the PCL's finest batters, Sheely was non-pareil in 1928, leading Sacramento's offense with an incredible .381 batting average.

While Sheely was the primary headline-grabber for the team that season, they made an even bigger acquisition on March 1 when a diminutive left-handed pitcher by the name of Tony Freitas was signed thanks to his dazzling success in the San Francisco Winter League. A California native by way of Mill Valley, Freitas would become arguably the franchise's all-time signature player, racking up one Sacramento baseball pitching record after another over the course of 15 seasons.

As if rewarding their fans with a championship wasn't reason enough to win, the Sacramento Senators were motivated further by an additional prize: $15,000, promised by the PCL to whichever club claimed the league title. They responded accordingly, winning consistently for the first two months of the season thanks to Sheely's dynamite bat.

The team had just ascended to first when the worst possible injury occurred on May 22. An errant pitch broke the little finger on Sheely's right hand, and the team responded by losing six in a row. The entire month of June was a slaughter, tumbling all the way to fifth place. They managed to scramble up to third by the time the first half of the season concluded on July 1, trailing San Francisco and Hollywood.

Moreing, determined as ever to see his team finally deliver a true winner, made a flurry of moves to revamp them for the second half. Underachieving pitchers were shipped off to other teams, while major league and PCL veteran righty James "Doc" Crandall was signed to boost the pitching staff. The overhaul clearly worked, as Sacramento roared to a 17-5 mark to commence the second half and reclaimed first place in August.

But the Hollywood Sheiks were hot on their trail, and by the time the two clubs met for a seven-game stand on September 11, the Senators were trailing their Southern California rivals by three games. Furthermore, they had to make up the deficit by playing all seven games in Wrigley Field in Los Angeles. But this club had a tenacity much unlike previous Senators teams, which they proved immediately and resoundingly. Crandall stifled Hollywood in the opening game, while Ray Keating shut them out the next one.

The offense took center stage in game three, amassing 19 hits and 13 runs to move into a first-place tie. The next day was the exact opposite, a nail-biter that spanned 16 innings. But Sacramento came through for a 6-5 victory, with Albert "Pudgy" Gould pitching an incredible 13 innings in relief.

Hollywood finally took a game on Saturday, but Sacramento rebounded by taking that Sunday's doubleheader to secure a two-game lead for first place. With seamless execution in both pitching and offense, the Senators had taken six of seven games in Los Angeles, a far cry from previous Sacramento teams that threatened first place down the stretch but ultimately faded.

Almost as soon as they had excelled in Los Angeles, however, it looked like the 1928 Senators would end up yet another bridesmaid. Just after their incredible stand in the City of Angels, they lost five of seven in San Francisco, leading to a tie for first between the two clubs as Hollywood faded in the final week. It all came down to a three-game playoff in early October to decide who would take first place for the second half, commencing at Moreing Field. In order to keep local fans up to the minute on the action, *The Sacramento Bee* hung an interactive baseball diamond outside its office building, showing every out, ball, strike, and baserunner as the game unfolded. The Senators did not disappoint, defeating the Seals 6-1 in the first game.

The action shifted to Recreation Park in San Francisco for game two, where the Senators homered their way to a 10-7 victory that crowned them the champions of the second half, the first PCL championship of any kind in Sacramento baseball history. Due to different formatting for the season, however, it wasn't the end of PCL play in 1928, as the league hosted its first championship playoff series in 23 years. It would be the first true championship postseason series any Sacramento ballclub had ever participated in.

The evenly matched squads commenced the seven-game competition on October 10, in San Francisco. The Senators pounced with yet another offensive blitz, notching 19 hits off of Seals starting pitcher Dutch Ruether. San Francisco withstood the assault for a 12-5 victory, but Sacramento responded the next day with an eventful 8-7 win. Not only did Sacramento's Claude Rohwer hit a grand slam, but the Seals pitcher who surrendered it, Elmer Jacobs, took out his frustration by hurling a ball at one-armed umpire Henry Fanning. Despite severely injuring Fanning's knee, Jacobs got off with a fine rather than a suspension.

After trading off wins in the next two contests, the series was tied at two games apiece at the outset of game five in San Francisco on Sunday. However, many Sacramentans were distracted by the opening of Hughes

Stadium at Sacramento Junior College, perhaps for the better as the Senators were shelled by the Seals 15-3. It was back to the River City for game six, which started promisingly for the home team as the Senators chased Dutch Ruether by the fourth inning.

Despite a 5-4 lead in the sixth inning, however, the usually steadfast arms of Gould and Crandall failed to close things out, and the Seals rallied to win the championship 9-5. Thus, they earned $9,000 of the PCL's promised $15,000. Despite not claiming the playoff title, the team could savor another silver lining in addition to their loser's share: extra money from postseason ticket sales, on top of a mountain of revenue generated during the regular season by a record 236,700 attendance.

With bountiful fan support and a season of unprecedented winning, Lew Moreing's Sacramento Senators looked like a model baseball franchise. *The Sporting News*, the leading sports publication in the United States, declared: "Sacramento is certainly right near the top, if not actually the best baseball city for its size in the country." It was a claim that could be empirically supported, as the team's total attendance for 1928 was two and a half times that of its population of 90,000 citizens.

Unfortunately, 1929 wouldn't continue the franchise's upward ascension. An up and down decade for the Senators ended on a resounding low note. Despite boasting future MLB stars like Dolph Camilli and nearby Davis native Myril Hoag amidst a lineup that was almost the same as 1928, the team quickly dropped to sixth place by the end of April. Worse was the status of Lew Moreing himself, as his brother (and co-owner) Charles passed away suddenly from an illness at a Sacramento hospital in April.

The team's constant losing only frustrated Moreing further. After a 10-game skid, he benched shortstop Ray French and released first baseman Joe Harris, but the team continued to trudge along at sixth place. Moreing did, however, successfully lobby for a significant change in PCL season play. He proposed a split season format, which was supported by the top brass of San Francisco's two clubs as well as Los Angeles and Portland. It allowed teams to be crowned the champion of either or both halves of the season, with a $10,000 prize to be split amongst the top five teams.

When the second half of the season commenced with four straight losses to the Hollywood Sheiks, Moreing made the familiar threat to sell or move the team. This time, that threat had more credence than ever before, as the gate receipts were paltry. A far cry from the nationally renowned attendance figures the season before, so few people came to the ballpark that during one week Moreing didn't even have sufficient funds to pay stadium workers, let alone the Senators themselves.

Fearing financial insolvency for himself as well as the team, Moreing quickly relinquished top players Hank Severeid and Doc Crandall to shed their high salaries. An injury to Dolph Camilli only hastened his consideration of selling the rest of the franchise. Several PCL owners were opposed to the idea of Sacramento losing its only ballclub, and even when former Seattle owner Charles Lockhart showed interest in buying the Senators, it was with the intent of keeping them in California's capital.

Unsurprisingly, the team's abysmal performance and Moreing's exhausted attempts to sell them hurt attendance. With so many regular players mortgaged off, home games at Moreing Field began to resemble sparsely attended practice sessions. They might as well have been, given how many temporary replacement players suited up for Sacramento in a penny-pinching maneuver by Moreing. Yet these cost-cutting measures didn't help him in his bid to sell the club, as a potential deal with a group from Long Beach (led by former Cubs pitcher Orval Overall) was derailed by Los Angeles Angels officials.

FOUR

1930S: GREAT DEPRESSION AND NIGHT BASEBALL

The precipitous drop from postseason play to just above last place and threats of being sold was no doubt harsh for Sacramento baseball fans to take. But when the calendar flipped to 1930, any headlines regarding baseball were far exceeded by the country's forthcoming economic woes. The stock market crashed on "Black Tuesday" in October 1929, bringing a shocking end to the speculative boom of the '20s and signaling the beginning of the Great Depression.

Given how thoroughly the Depression would ravage pivotal industries like automobiles and farming, baseball was unsurprisingly hit hard as well. Many teams, as well as entire leagues, were put out of business, ushering legions of players into the many winding bread lines across the country.

For Sacramento baseball fans, any threat of losing their Senators to the Depression were preceded by Lew Moreing's increasing efforts to sell them in the first place. While he ultimately didn't follow through on that threat, he nonetheless continued his 1929 model of assembling the team for as cheap as possible. In 1930, he at least made the effort to sign local players like journeyman catcher Elwood "Kettle" Wirts and 17-year-old prospect

Hank Steinbacher. Those two would excel, as opposed to underwhelming scrap heap acquisitions like Aaron Ward and Wally Hood who didn't even make it to the end of the season.

Yet the most enduring development of 1930 wouldn't come from any player's performance, or even the Depression. Moreing had been kicking around an idea for two years, and it was time to bring it to fruition: night baseball games. Prior to 1930, the very thought of taking the field after sundown was largely scoffed at in baseball, only being tried a handful of times.

Now, however, it was clearly an idea whose time had come. The Des Moines Demons of the Class A Western League installed lighting and played their first night game on May 2. What usually would have been an obscure local sporting event became a national spectacle, with MLB Commissioner Kenesaw Mountain Landis attending and audiences across the country tuning into NBC's radio broadcast of the game.

Moreing was not only savvy in emulating another entrepreneurial owner, but also economical. He realized many working-class fans couldn't attend weekday games, a detail all the more important in the midst of the job-strapped Depression. He quickly ordered poles and lights before setting the Senators' June 10 home game against the Oakland Oaks as the first ever Pacific Coast League night game. Especially in such close proximity to the beginning of summer, it was an ideal, picturesque time to make history.

Of course, it was one that needed preparation. With the Senators still on a road trip, Moreing tested the lights on June 5 with backup players who weren't traveling with the team. At 8:31 PM, with hundreds of onlookers crowding around outside the stadium, 40 lights perched on four towering wooden poles instantly emitted 180,000 watts of light across every inch of Moreing Field.

The local media was abuzz with excitement over the instant success of such an ambitious technological leap. "The first ball pitched...met the hitter's bat for a long drive into center field," raved Steve George of *The Sacramento Union*. "The ball was visible from the time it left the pitcher's hand until it fell smack against the centerfielder's glove." His verdict: "Lew Moreing's $10,000 gamble was a success. Old Sol was never more neatly eclipsed by the moon than he is by the new lights at Moreing Field." Such words were no doubt music to the ears of Lew Moreing after pouring so much money into a risky adventure during such financially stringent times.

On June 10, the first ever night game in Sacramento baseball history unfolded as planned. Although the total attendance was a few thousand smaller than expected, this wasn't due to lack of fan interest, but strangely because of it; as it turned out, many stayed home out of worry they wouldn't be able to get in as a result of the expected massive crowd. Nonetheless, the Senators didn't disappoint those who did show up, easily trouncing the Oaks in an 8-0 victory.

The towering lights that illuminated the field weren't the only technological first that night. Sacramento's flagship radio station KFBK (which was owned by the McClatchy newspapers), despite being on the air since 1922, had completely ignored the Senators for years. But the novelty of Moreing Field's brand-new lights quickly changed their minds. While the Senators blanked the Oaks, announcer Ernie Smith and *Sacramento Bee* sports editor Rudy Hickey took to the airwaves to describe the action, as well as the pre-game festivities.

It was a historic moment not only as the first night game in Sacramento baseball history, but in PCL history as well. League president Harry Williams and officials from other teams were on hand to witness, and were quickly convinced of the advantages of night baseball. Sure enough, the Senators would be the opposing team for the nighttime debuts of Wrigley Field in Los Angeles on July 22 and Emeryville Ballpark in Oakland on August 5. Seattle and Portland added lights during the 1930 season as well, while San Francisco's two clubs christened the new Seals Stadium with lights the next year. Altogether, the PCL far preceded Major League Baseball in welcoming night baseball, as the majors wouldn't host an after-dusk contest until 1935.

Not surprisingly, the advent of night baseball sent attendance soaring, just as Moreing expected. By midseason, their total attendance was 4,200 more than 1929, and finished at 219,300 by season's end (the second highest in Sacramento history). Hollywood owner Bill Lane, originally averse to the idea of night games, changed his mind and praised the Senators: "Instead of being the weak sister of the league, Sacramento now is one of the best drawing towns in the circuit and is second only to Los Angeles."

Attendance wasn't the only thing boosted by night play; the team's performance surged accordingly. They managed to jump into first place over the next two weeks after the June 10 night debut, but a seven-game sweep by the Hollywood Sheiks sent them into a tumble to third place. It's ultimately where they would stay in the second half, trailing both Hollywood and Los Angeles.

While they didn't attain the postseason heights of 1928, the 1930 Sacramento Senators were still a solid team anchored by several standout performances. The most esteemed player on the roster was Myril Hoag, a native of nearby Davis who would go on to aid four New York Yankees championship teams throughout the decade. In 1930, he led the offense in almost every category, including batting average (.337), runs (148), hits (244), doubles (57), and RBIs (121). On the pitcher's mound, Tony Freitas quickly ascended to ace status with a team-best 19 wins, 3.24 ERA, and four shutouts. Fay Thomas led in every other pitching category, amassing 298 innings and 228 strikeouts.

As the 1931 season approached, the Great Depression worsened, and Moreing continued to assemble the Senators at the cheapest price possible. Yet just because players were signing for cheap didn't mean they were of a commensurate subpar quality. This approach had netted fast-rising young stars like Tony Freitas and Dolph Camilli, as well as promising reserve out-fielder Hank Steinbacher.

One of Moreing's discount acquisitions for 1931 was a 21-year-old banker and Sacramento native named Stan Hack, who would become perhaps the greatest player ever to hail from the city. In 1931, he slashed an eye-popping .352 batting average, 232 hits, 128 runs, and 13 triples, while stealing 20 bases. To no one's surprise, he was sold right afterward to the Chicago Cubs, where he wove a Hall of Fame-worthy career that included four trips to the World Series.

Yet Hack's sensational year belied the team's overall quality. Thanks in part to a large spate of injuries, they finished second to last in the first half, and third to last in the second. Their offense aside from Hack was often anemic, suffering the indignity of being no-hit twice. Pitching wunderkind Tony Freitas, despite a season where he led the staff in almost every single category, was arrested in August for speeding in his hometown of Mill Valley, losing his car for 30 days and spending five days in jail as punishment. Even then, he still had a better year than the rest of the staff, with Ed Bryan and Tom Flynn both losing 18 games.

After such a dip in quality for the team, Moreing attempted another fire sale. Hack went to Chicago for $50,000, and while he courted five teams to acquire Freitas, none would meet his asking price. The cash from the Hack deal was especially necessary given 1931's attendance was less than half what it was the previous season. The novelty of night baseball had clearly been overshadowed by the team's drop in the standings, and the ever-worsening economic conditions of the Depression didn't help matters.

Things only got worse in 1932. Attendance sank to a paltry 68,400 fans, a significant portion of which came on Opening Day. Given that over a third of Sacramento's entire population was unemployed, it wasn't much of a surprise. The team's performance didn't help matters, skidding into sixth place by May despite a promising first two weeks. The most consistent bright spot was the impeccable pitching of Freitas, who pitched the PCL's first ever nighttime no-hitter on May 5, his 24th birthday. Weeks later, Moreing finally saw an offer for his prized left-hander he deemed sufficient when Philadelphia Athletics manager-owner Connie Mack ponied up $25,000 and a pitcher.

Disappointing as it was for fans to suddenly say goodbye to "Tiny Tony," the pitcher they got in exchange, Jimmy DeShong, performed even better. With a sterling 19-6 record, a team-best 3.16 ERA, and fewer hits surrendered than innings pitched, he put together one of the best seasons by a pitcher in franchise history. Unsurprisingly, he was purchased before season's end by the New York Yankees. The team's other marquee performer for the year, outfielder Frank Demaree, ended up joining Stan Hack in Chicago for an undisclosed amount.

The season's most intriguing development came when they acquired Earl McNeely, the native son of the early '20s who became a World Series hero for the Washington Senators. At a price tag of just $3,000, he was hardly the high-priced star Moreing had sold to Washington in 1924. But he was still a crucial acquisition, and not just because of his solid .281 batting average; he became the club's manager on August 4 when Buddy Ryan inexplicably quit the position.

Despite much success as both a player and a manager for Sacramento, Ryan had become exhausted by the demands of managerial duties as well as outside business priorities, chiefly the Sacramento gas station chain he owned. Yet this wasn't the whole of the story, as it was later revealed he had gone unpaid for several seasons and was doing the job out of friendly respect for Lew Moreing. Fortunately, he received compensation after bringing his case to MLB Commissioner Kenesaw Mountain Landis.

As it turned out, Ryan's departure proved a galvanic turning point for the team. With McNeely at the helm, they rattled off series wins over Hollywood, San Francisco and Oakland to reach .500. A 10-game winning streak lifted them to third place, where they stood at season's end with 101 wins. Their offense was their greatest asset, with Dolph Camilli leading almost every category and Frank Demaree, Hank Steinbacher, Frenchy Bordagaray and Larry Woodall also batting over .300.

Even more newsworthy than McNeely's return and the offense was a historic pitching duel that took place against Oakland at the end of the season. Moreing signed a Japanese-American pitcher named Kenso Nushida, the first player of Japanese heritage in PCL history. Yet Moreing wasn't exactly Branch Rickey; his motives were largely commercial, knowing Nushida's presence on the team would attract the patronage of the thousands of Japanese who lived in California.

Nushida was no Tony Freitas, ending up with an ERA of 5.00. But sure enough, the seats were jam-packed every time he pitched. As the year was winding down, Moreing concocted a brilliant publicity stunt with Oakland Oaks owner Victor Devincenzi. Oakland had signed a local Chinese pitcher named Lee Gum Hong, setting up a Japan vs. China showdown that was sure to grab headlines and fill the stands.

Much like the Joe Louis-Max Schmeling boxing rivalry that same decade, it tapped into a deeper national conflict, as Japan and China had been military foes since the first Sino-Japanese War in 1894. In September 1931, a year before Moreing and Devincenzi's ethnically charged showcase, Japan occupied Manchuria to create a puppet government to global condemnation.

While far less incendiary than a military occupation, the matchup drew intense fan interest. 3,000 fans (the largest crowd Oakland had entertained in months) turned out expecting a duel, only for Nushida to tire after 4⅓ innings and three runs allowed. But relief pitcher Laurie Vinci saved the day by lacing a bases-loaded triple off Hong for a 7-5 comeback win. Hong evened the score four days later in the season's final game, out-dueling

Nushida for a 7-1 complete game victory. Five years after Nushida and Hong's amicable pitching duels, Japan launched a full-scale invasion of China just before the outset of World War II.

Despite 101 wins, brilliant hitting and an intriguing ethnic pitching battle, attendance continued to dwindle. The Senators welcomed less than 69,000 patrons all season, although every other team in the PCL was witnessing a similar drop in attendance. PCL officials and owners agreed during the offseason to cut ticket prices in half, but Moreing refused. He set rates of 85 cents for the reserved sections and 60 cents for grandstand seats, while agreeing to the 25 cents rate for bleachers (all with federal tax included).

The 1933 Sacramento Senators were almost identical in terms of roster composition and cheap price tag. Moreing was so thorough in his cost-cutting ways by now that he even moved spring training from the Richardson Springs spa to Moreing Field. Earl McNeely stayed as manager, while also playing in the outfield. As if he had dipped into a fountain of youth, he looked like his 1924 self through the first 40 games with an eye-popping .444 average that was even higher than those of Woodall, Bordagaray, Camilli and Steinbacher. Standing in first at May, the team faltered in August and dropped to fourth, yet still won a solid 96 games.

But as far as attendance was concerned, the song remained the same for the Senators and the PCL as a whole. The familiar threat of the Solons being sold to new ownership reared its head when real estate magnates Harry Kronich and John "Foghorn" Murphy came to Northern California in the hopes of buying a team. After their effort to acquire the Oakland Oaks went nowhere, they came to Moreing with an offer of $125,000 maximum to buy the Senators. Moreing offered the team and the field wholesale for $250,000, but the two wanted to lease instead of own the park, and the deal fell through.

As it turned out, new ownership might have been preferable. An October report by *The Sacramento Bee* revealed that the team's players hadn't been paid since August 15, leading many of them to file for MLB free agency. As he had done many times before, Moreing opted for a fire sale of his best players, including Larry Woodall, Frenchy Bordagaray, and Leroy Hermann, with Dolph Camilli already shipped off to Chicago.

As it turned out, it was the end of the road for the Lew Moreing era. For almost a decade and a half, Moreing had been the longest-serving owner in franchise history. He took them to new heights with the acquisition of some of the finest players in Sacramento history, modernized their stadium, instigated PCL firsts like night baseball and the league's first Japanese pitcher, and oversaw the team's first ever playoff series.

But the Great Depression wasn't sparing him, and his inability to pay players was just the tip of the iceberg. He also had other investments, chiefly in agricultural enterprises. But the Senators and Moreing Field were his most successful financial holdings by far, often serving as collateral when he took out loans for other endeavors and assisting friends and family in need.

In February of 1934, the banks holding those loans came calling to the tune of $160,000. Moreing, as had been the case so many times through the Senators' frequent financial woes, figured he would be bailed out by other financiers. But that assistance didn't materialize by the banks' February 13 afternoon deadline, and Moreing's absence in San Francisco at 3 P.M. that day didn't go unnoticed. *The Oakland Tribune* ran a headline that very day: **"Deadline 3 P.M., Where Is Moreing With Cash?"** The article noted he had attended the PCL owners meeting in Oakland the prior month, where he could have easily asked for financial assistance.

Nonetheless, he never showed, and all of Moreing's holdings in the team were foreclosed. The banks thus assumed financial control of the Sacramento Senators franchise. While it was a sad end to a consistent era of ownership, this changing of the guard would soon lead to even greater heights of prestige for professional baseball in Sacramento.

FIVE

DAWN OF THE CARDINAL YEARS

As the 1934 season commenced, Lew Moreing was out after years of owner-ship. Various California banks were now in control of the franchise, with Earl McNeely selected as its de facto president. McNeely was the perfect choice, being a native of Sacramento, one of the team's greatest ever players, and a World Series hero in the major leagues.

When a new owner or executive takes the reins of a baseball team, it's imperative they make moves that immediately signify the direction they intend to take it. McNeely wasted no time showing he planned to run the team frugally, albeit in a manner a bit more flexible than Moreing. Basically, he was willing to sell any players necessary, even if it was for a price far less than what his predecessor had demanded for them.

First to go was first baseman George Kelly, followed by Frenchy Bordagaray's sale to the Chicago White Sox for $12,500. But Chicago would "return to sender" before the summer even started, for while he was a phenomenal hitter, his fielding was proportionally terrible. Pitcher Laurie Vinci and outfielder Cal Lahman were released during the season to save even more money.

The 1934 season was more like a tale of two seasons in one. The first half was reasonably successful, holding third place thanks primarily to stellar pitching. Attendance, in steady decline due to the Depression and inconsistent play, saw an improvement thanks to savvy moves by McNeely. The old policy of letting women attend for free on certain days, scrapped by Moreing to cut costs, was reinstated. Parking fees behind the left field wall were eliminated, and reservations for every section except box seats were lifted on weekdays.

The second half, however, couldn't have been any worse. The Senators' anemic offense soon overrode their strong pitching, and they tumbled into last place almost instantly. Attendance depleted accordingly, and McNeely started to look like Lew Moreing by cancelling all night games in order to save money.

After only one season, McNeely was quick to discover the harsh realities of keeping a professional baseball club financially solvent. After appointing catcher Kettle Wirts as manager, McNeely shifted his attention exclusively to front office dealings. It was fortunate for McNeely's personal well-being he relinquished the managerial reigns, as 1935 turned out to be an unmitigated disaster for the club. By June 1, they were in dead last, and Wirts was fired. The offense did well, but was overshadowed by subpar pitching, with only one starter posting a winning record.

Attendance once again slipped, sinking as low as 400 during a game against the first place Angels. Just like the Moreing era, moving the team was back on the table. McNeely received an inquiry about moving them to San Diego, all while he continued to desperately sell off players left and right. The club finished second-to-last in both halves of the season.

Yet there was no greater loss during the season than that of Moreing himself. The erstwhile owner who shaped the franchise suddenly died of a heart attack at his home in Barstow in June. Still in financial destitution, he had invested in a gold mine in his hometown in hopes of recovering his losses at the time of his passing. On June 17, the current team, as well as some former players, played a benefit game for his widow Edith, and raised almost $3,000 for her.

One positive did emerge from the dreck of the 1935 season: a new name. After years of being known as the Sacramento Senators, many fans started referring to the team as the Solons, a moniker that had steadily gained traction for years. Senators, while appropriate for a team in a capital city, was fairly conventional given it was also used by MLB's Washington franchise. Solons, on the other hand, maintained the legislative imagery with a much less employed phrase. The word derived from Solon of Ancient Greece, an Athenian lawmaker regarded for his efforts to legislatively address many societal issues.

Yet even a clever new name wasn't enough to stem the familiar tide of seemingly insurmountable financial troubles. As the season wound down, California banking superintendent George Walker filed a breach of loan notice against the team on the order of $50,000. If it wasn't paid by December 18, the ballpark would be foreclosed on. Earl McNeely commenced his most desperate fire sale yet, auctioning off eight players.

After years of penny-pinching, selling top players, paltry attendance, and threats of moving or contraction, the team now had a strict deadline to resolve all of it. Fortunately, the Sacramento Solons found salvation from an unlikely, albeit prestigious, source. On December 12, six days before Walker's threatened foreclosure, McNeely received a phone call early in the morning. It was Bill Killefer, a former coach for MLB's St. Louis Cardinals. Killefer informed him that Cardinals president Sam Breadon wanted to buy the team but needed an answer by noon.

McNeely immediately contacted the Sacramento Chamber of Commerce's baseball committee, who contacted the Merchants Bank (the official owners of the club) insisting they donate it to the Cardinals for the benefit of Sacramento. The bank refused and demanded a $5,000 asking price to acquire the franchise. Killefer and the chamber worked out a deal, and just like that, the St. Louis Cardinals owned the Sacramento Solons.

Being a minor league affiliate for a major league franchise in and of itself was a much-needed relief for Sacramento. But being the affiliate for the St. Louis Cardinals was no ordinary affiliation. The Cardinals had become one of the sport's elite organizations in the past decade, winning five National League pennants and three World Series titles, including the previous year of 1934.

Moreover, St. Louis's perennial success was a direct product of their peerless farm system. Featuring 10 teams, it had produced a parade of superlative players like Pepper Martin, Dizzy Dean and Joe Medwick, and later churned out Stan Musial, Enos Slaughter and Billy Southworth. Pioneered by general manager Branch Rickey (later the man who signed Jackie Robinson to the Brooklyn Dodgers), this format of multiple teams serving one major league club created the model for farm systems still used by MLB franchises today.

The Solons were now a crucial part of that farm system, albeit not without protest from other PCL owners. Many feared that Sacramento would overpower the rest of the league with St. Louis's abundance of talent and resources. At the beginning of 1936, PCL directors issued a new rule that prohibited the sale or trade of player from any Class AA team after August 1 without that player passing through waivers.

Rickey and farm director Phillip G. Bartelme approved of the rule, and the Sacramento Solons were now securely under the ownership of the St. Louis Cardinals. The only thing left to resolve was the foreclosure sale of Moreing Field, which St. Louis opted to lease for five years for a total of $16,000, in addition to spending $5,000 to renovate it.

After years of tumultuous ownership changes and threats thereof, exacerbated chiefly by the Great Depression, the Sacramento Solons were now in their surest hands yet. Rickey, a consummate baseball pioneer and future Hall of Famer, immediately appointed Phil Bartelme as team president and Bill Killefer as manager. Sacramento fans used to the volatility of personnel changes over the years, as well as ownership that frequently threatened to sell or fold, had to feel good about the prospects of stability going forward with these hires. The ballpark was even renamed Cardinal Field in tribute to their new overseers.

Rickey's first approach to building the actual roster, however, was far less sure-handed. He decided to assemble the 1936 Solons by holding tryouts for semi-pros and amateurs, a move he admitted was a shocking deviation from anything he had ever tried before. PCL owners and officials were deeply skeptical of Rickey's plan, considering it a scheme; league president W.C. Tuttle issued a reminder that the PCL constitution required a minimum of 15 players on each roster with at least Class A experience (the Solons were Class AA).

It didn't help that Rickey wasn't exactly expecting a pennant winner in the first place. In a surprising moment of honesty, Rickey eschewed rosy promises of a winning team at a town hall with fans on March 12, in Sacramento. Fans were hungry for a winner after several losing seasons and understandably expected an immediate improvement by being in the St. Louis farm system. But Rickey assured them the winning would come in due time. "Cardinal farm teams have won 24 pennants in nine years, and I expect the Sacramento club will be added to the list," he proclaimed.

A Solons scorecard from 1942, with the Cardinals logo prominently displayed. The affiliation with St. Louis was as beneficial to Sacramento's brand as it was to the quality of the team. Photo courtesy of Alan O'Connor.

However, Rickey's sober forecast for the 1936 season would come true first. The Solons, now officially bearing the name after a fan vote in the *Sacramento Union*, lost 111 games and finished dead last. This could largely be chalked up to their roster, with many players conditioned in places like Columbus, Cedar Rapids and Council Bluffs, but had never donned the cleats for a Pacific Coast League squad. Attendance barely topped the previous year, and nicknames like "Killefer's Kiddies" and "the sockless Solons" appeared in the papers.

Fans craved better results for 1937, which necessitated another roster shakeup by Branch Rickey. Rather than an amateur tryout, the first big move was a welcome one: former Sacramento ace Tony Freitas was shipped back to his old team from Columbus. The team was rounded out by other acquisitions like hard-throwing left-handed pitcher Tom Seats, catcher William Walker Cooper and shortstop Joe Orengo.

These moves had many PCL managers and baseball journalists predicting a worst-to-first season for the Solons. Radio broadcaster and former Sacramento pitcher Walter Mails dubbed them "the team to beat," while Portland manager Bill Sweeney effused, "I can't see how the Solons can miss being in the first division and playoffs." Rickey himself had promised fans in the town hall of March 1936 that the Solons would soon join the extensive lineage of winning Cardinals farm teams. He reiterated that promise a few months later in July while visiting Killefer and Bartelme, saying the team would contend for a pennant the very next year.

Sure enough, the 1937 team lived up to the anticipation with 102 wins and a first-place finish. Their powerful offense was anchored by veteran infielder Art Garibaldi's .327 average, in addition to being one of five players with double-digit home run totals. Tony Freitas, meanwhile, anchored the pitching with an incredible return season. He won 23 games, the most of anyone on the staff, and also posted a team-best 290 innings pitched, 2.86 ERA, and 108 strikeouts (the last stat tied with Bob Klinger). Attendance soared accordingly, totaling 144,000, their best in seven years.

Most important, however, was Sacramento's first postseason appearance since 1928. Especially as the AA affiliate of a team with three recent World Series titles, fans expected a championship Sacramento could call its own. Their opponent in the PCL playoff was San Diego, who had slumped towards the end of the regular season. Given the first three games of the best-of-seven were to be played at Cardinal Field, the stage seemed to be set for the Solons to cruise to a title.

A San Francisco native who started his PCL career with the Seals, Art Garibaldi fueled the 1937 Solons with a robust average and many home runs. He played several other seasons for Sacramento, and later worked as a bartender at Sacramento's Pal's Club after baseball. Photo courtesy of Alan O'Connor.

However, it wasn't meant to be. Despite sending Freitas to the mound in games one and four, the Solons were swept by San Diego in four games. But if it was any consolation, they received a loser's share of $3,750 that was distributed evenly to the players. Especially after the time Moreing couldn't pay his own players during the cost-cutting days a few years before, this was a welcome change of circumstance for the club.

Having come close, only to finish with a disappointing playoff sweep, the Solons entered 1938 determined to go all the way. But before they could even face any adversity on the diamond, an unexpected obstacle threatened their plans in February. A violent windstorm hit Sacramento, destroying the grandstand roof and entrance of Cardinal Field and requiring $10,000 in repairs.

Extensive damage was done to the grand-stand at Cardinal Field by yesterday's severe windstorm. The picture shows the debris strewn front entrance. *Bee Photo*

A *Sacramento Bee* **photo showing the ravages of the February 1938 windstorm that hit Cardinal Field. Photo courtesy of Alan O'Connor.**

Luckily, the season was able to proceed without delay, commencing with Tony Freitas besting Oakland at Cardinal Field. It set the tone for a season where pitching consistently led the team, led by Freitas' 24 wins, 159 strikeouts and 2.67 ERA. However, the potent offense that launched 110 home runs the year before was oddly inconsistent in 1938. With Garibaldi having been promoted to St. Louis, the offense lumbered to a .209 collective average to start the year.

Adding further adversity was the health of manager Bill Killefer. In late April, the 50-year-old skipper was hospitalized for six weeks after experiencing inability to eat or sleep. He was diagnosed with jaundice, missing the rest of the season as a result. With Doc Crandall filling in for Killefer, the Solons managed to play even better, reaching first place by late May as their impeccable rotation made up for the listless offense.

The Solons continued their first-place tear into late June, with a seemingly insurmountable seven-game lead. However, two lopsided series losses to the Los Angeles Angels sent them into a minor stumble to third place. Fortunately, it was still good enough to qualify for the playoffs. They drew Los Angeles as their first-round opponent, which likely had fans fearing a repeat of the San Diego sweep in the 1937 playoff. In 27 head-to-head regular season matchups with the Angels, the Solons had only taken six.

Yet it hardly played out that way. The Solons took two of the first three games in Los Angeles, then two of the next three to win the series. They advanced to the next round to face San Francisco, this time getting to commence the action at Cardinal Field. The Solons did not disappoint, scoring 37 runs (including 22 in the third game) to win the President's Cup and a $5,000 winner's share.

It was fortunate the Solons claimed a postseason prize in 1938, as they would go through 1939 with a relatively green manager at the helm. Killefer, exhausted by his health issues, stepped down permanently and was replaced by Bernard "Benny" Borgmann. Borgmann possessed no previous PCL experience, and had only managed several clubs in the lower echelons of the Cardinals farm system. The move was even more head-scratching given Phil Bartelme also strongly considered the more qualified Burleigh Grimes, a future Hall of Famer who had just managed the Brooklyn Dodgers for two seasons.

Many fans and sportswriters were skeptical of the hire. Branch Rickey added to the negative publicity when he said in March that the team "won't do as a pennant contender as things stand now." Sounding more like a sports columnist than a stately executive, he claimed they had "no color, no pep, not even any chatter." It didn't help when the Solons lost their first 10 games, all of them played at home. It wasn't all Borgmann's fault, as the roster was comparably unfamiliar due to the shuffling of players to St. Louis by Rickey. Garibaldi and Freitas returned, but the awful start extended well into late June with the Solons sitting at last place.

However, Sacramento suddenly did a mirror image of the season's beginning by winning 10 straight at home, lifting them to fourth place and sending attendance soaring. The year's total would end up at 116,700, a vast improvement over 1938. Fans were primarily enthralled by Tony Freitas' 38 consecutive scoreless innings pitched, breaking the PCL mark of 36 by Jimmy Whalen of the San Francisco Seals in 1905. They remained at fourth place by season's end at a respectable 88-88, far better than their dreadful beginning put them on pace for.

Most importantly, they managed to place just enough to qualify for the President's Cup playoffs once again. The Solons dispatched San Francisco in five games to face Los Angeles, who had finished third in the regular season but defeated first-place Seattle in their first series. The Angels won the opener at Cardinal Field 2-1, but Sacramento sent fans home happy with victories in the next two games. The action shifted to Los Angeles, where the Solons won two of the next three to claim their second consecutive President's Cup playoff.

After the financial destitution and inconsistent play that marred the end of the Lew Moreing era, the Sacramento Solons ended the 1930s with their most stable ownership setup yet, which quickly produced a first-place finish and two consecutive playoff title victories immediately after. The 1940s, a decade that saw even more regal success for the Cardinals, would bring the Solons their greatest glory...as well as further tribulation.

SIX

1940S: FROM THE CELLAR TO THE PENNANT...AND BACK AGAIN

The dawn of the 1940s, much like the beginning of the previous decade, was defined by world events far bigger than baseball. In the fall of 1939, around the time the Solons were heading for another playoff title, Nazi Germany invaded Poland, officially commencing World War II. In June of 1940, Adolf Hitler's ruthless Panzer divisions conquered France.

Unlike the Great Depression at the outset of the '30s, however, the impact hadn't reached the U.S. just yet. Baseball continued unperturbed for the moment, and Solons fans in particular expected another postseason run to commence the new decade. But 1940 would demonstrate the sobering reality of being a minor league affiliate, as Branch Rickey constantly cycled players throughout St. Louis's vast farm system all year long.

The usually reliable Art Garibaldi experienced a down year and was unwillingly shipped to San Diego in July. First baseman Larry Barton's similarly underwhelming bat sent him to Columbus. Luckily, fan favorite Tony Freitas wasn't traded away, although he led the staff in unfavorable categories like runs allowed and losses. Injuries only made things worse, with outfielder Dick Lang and infielder Roy Pfleger both suffering broken legs.

The end result was 90 wins and a fifth-place finish, a disappointing follow-up to back-to-back President's Cup wins.

After a mediocre season, Rickey unsurprisingly opted to hire a new manager to galvanize the club. His choice was an outstanding one: John "Pepper" Martin. Memorably nicknamed "The Wild Horse of Osage," Martin distinguished himself as a member of the Cardinals' "Gashouse Gang" championship teams of the '30s. As a player, his aggressive baserunning, head-first slides, and nimble outfield work earned him comparisons to Ty Cobb. Most importantly, he was the key factor in St. Louis's upset World Series victory over the Philadelphia Athletics in 1931.

For Martin, it was perfect timing. His relentlessly physical style of play ended up taking a severe toll on his body, necessitating retirement from the majors. But he was ready for a second act as a manager and could still handle minor league playing. When Rickey signed him as manager, Martin eagerly promised to bring "Gashouse Gang baseball" to the River City, in addition to patrolling right field. In February of 1941, Martin, accompanied by his wife, three daughters and two dogs, drove 1,600 miles from Oklahoma to their new rental home in Sacramento.

Accordingly, the roster was reshaped in a way that promised playoff contention. Tony Freitas once again led the pitching staff, supplemented by the likes of Bill Schmidt, Red Munger and Albert "Boots" Hollingsworth. New Orleans' hard-hitting shortstop Frank Scalzi was acquired in a big trade to fill the void left by Buddy Blattner's transition to second base. Newly acquired first baseman Maurice Sturdy's offense befit his surname, thanks to his .295 average with Columbus in 1940. Second was covered by Don Gutteridge, who possessed the kind of speed Martin sought to bring to the team just as he had in St. Louis.

Martin's first season proved to be as excellent as hoped. The 1941 Solons crackled with the kind of gritty energy and tenacity that defined the Gashouse Gang Cardinals. They stole bases at a dizzying clip, hustled for infield hits, and stupefied opposing defenses. Yet they weren't limited to just small ball, launching 41 home runs by June. The pitching was brilliant, not only in the ample starting rotation but the bullpen as well. The sports press raved about the team, with Will Connolly of the *San Francisco Chronicle* dubbing them "the most spectacular ball club to show in the Coast League in a long time." At the midpoint of June, they were a staggering 50-19, 14 games ahead in first place, and had already entertained over 100,000 fans. Eight players, Martin included, represented Sacramento at the PCL All-Star Game in San Francisco.

The second half would prove to be far less entertaining. A series of injuries and a slumping offense caused the team to lose 14 of their last 27 games when "Pepper Martin Night" occurred on July 11, at Cardinal Field. Despite the slump, the Solons remained 10 games ahead in first, and 14,300 showed up to shower their indefatigable manager with gifts and praise. With his wife at his side, an emotional Martin could barely speak as he surveyed a parade of gifts such as a 1941 Chrysler New Yorker four-door sedan, a shotgun, a hunting dog, and a new set of dishes.

Unfortunately, the joy of that night didn't last Martin the rest of the season. While driving his new vehicle with his wife on a night trip to Marysville, he was run off the road by another driver. Incensed, Martin walked up to the other vehicle and punched the driver, dislocating a finger in the process. The Solons went into a nosedive in August and September, suddenly losing games as profusely as they won them in the first half.

The end result was still a strong 102-75, but they finished second to Seattle. Similar to the '30s, the President's Cup playoff offered a chance to end the season on a strong note. They easily swept San Diego in the first round to meet Seattle, taking a 3-2 series lead thanks to the pitching of Freitas and Munger. But Seattle fought back valiantly to win the final two games, claiming the cup.

Just like in 1937, a postseason disappointment only served to whet Sacramento fans' appetite for even better results the next year. But the 1941 offseason would be greatly overshadowed by a shocking development in the war. On December 7, Japanese fighter pilots attacked the U.S. naval base at Pearl Harbor, Hawaii, and America finally entered the conflict. The growth of WWII had indeed been prevalent in people's minds all throughout 1941; *Sacramento Bee* sports writer Wilbur Adams likened the Solons' aggressive style of play to Hitler's Panzer divisions during the first half.

Even with the U.S. now officially in the war, baseball continued in Sacramento in 1942. Across the nation, the game was almost immediately impeded by the war effort. The U.S. government restricted the crowd size at all sporting events, fearing they could present an attractive target for enemy forces. Night games on the West Coast were eliminated in tandem with wartime power restrictions. MLB Commissioner Kenesaw Mountain Landis even contacted President Franklin D. Roosevelt asking whether baseball should go on in 1942, with Roosevelt insisting the game should continue for the country's morale.

An aerial photo of Cardinal Field, with Tower Theater nearby.
Photo courtesy of Alan O'Connor.

Luckily, the Solons were largely unaffected by the draft, and fielded a team as capable as their almost-champion the year prior. Tony Freitas and Bill Schmidt returned in the starting rotation, this time aided by Sylvester "Blix" Donnelly, Kemp Wicker and Clarence Beers. The outfield was entirely new, anchored by Tommy Thompson, Bill Shewey and Debs Garms. Infielder Eddie Lake, who had spent the previous three seasons with St. Louis, brought much needed depth. Ray Mueller, a cousin of 1941 second baseman Don Gutteridge, provided a sturdy presence behind the plate and another powerful bat. And of course, Pepper Martin led the way as player-manager once more.

Throughout the season, the Solons won consistently and hovered around first and second place. But more often than not, it seemed like 1942 was defined more by tribulation both on and off the field. The realities of the war were ever present, none grimmer than in May. Earlier in February, President Roosevelt signed Executive Order 9066, which ordered all Japanese Americans to be rounded up and sent to internment camps. On May 7, the U.S. Army ushered 3,800 people of Japanese descent into the halls of Memorial Auditorium for transfer to the prison at Tule Lake in Siskiyou County.

In July, the team dealt with a tragic loss when former catching prospect Jim Grilk suddenly died in an automobile accident in Woodland. While he wasn't playing for the Solons at the present time, he had been in Sacramento working as an athletic director at the Sacramento Army Air Base. Perhaps appropriately, the Solons dropped out of first place behind Los Angeles. Attendance was stagnant all season regardless, chiefly due to the lack of night games and the extended time commitment working in industry to create war goods.

As the season neared its final weekend, there seemed little reason to hope for a return to the playoffs. The final series was a seven-game home-stand at Cardinal Field, but it was against none other than Los Angeles. Predictably, the Angels won the first two games, putting Sacramento four games out of first with just five left to play. If the Solons wanted to claim their elusive first PCL pennant, they had to win every last game.

In the third game, the Solons lived to see another day thanks to an unlikely walk-off. In the bottom of the ninth, third baseman Steve Mesner scored the winning run when the Los Angeles defense threw away a routine double play. Given the fact that the Angels were the best fielding squad in the PCL, winning a game on an error by them was borderline miraculous. The next game on Friday was a standard pitching masterpiece by Freitas, while the offense backed him up with 17 hits and ten runs.

All of a sudden, the Solons trailed by just two games with three to play. The first was set for Saturday, and the last two as a doubleheader on Sunday. Saturday's game upped the drama considerably, going all the way to the 11th inning. The Angels took the lead in the top half, needing just three outs to clinch the pennant. But after a walk to Buster Adams, pinch hitter Gene Lillard slammed a home run for a 6-5 walk-off win.

Yet the drama was hardly over, as the Solons trailed late in the first game of Sunday's doubleheader. 11,600 fans at Cardinal Field watched their team head into the bottom of the eighth down 5-3. Suddenly, the Solons erupted for four runs, including a two-run homer by Ray Mueller. Freitas stepped into the fray in the ninth and sent the Angels down in order, officially tying for first place. Already warmed up sufficiently by closing out game one, Freitas then started game two, twirling a four-hit, 5-1 victory. Against all odds, the Sacramento Solons were undisputed PCL champions for the first time ever.

It was a spectacular finish in every way, one befitting of a baseball movie like *The Natural*. In a year where the grim specter of war loomed large and the team dealt with the death of a former player, the victory carried greater resonance. To sweeten things even further, the St. Louis Cardinals won their fourth World Series the very next month.

Tony Freitas (on the left) and manager Pepper Martin bask in the glory of the Solons' magical 1942 PCL championship, the first such title in franchise history. Photo courtesy of Alan O'Connor.

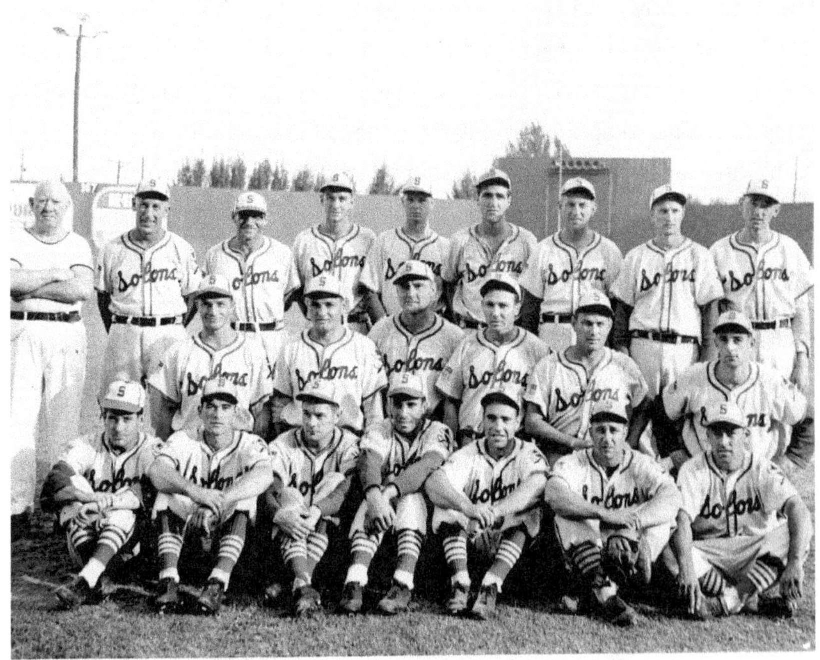

The 1942 Solons team photo. Photo courtesy of Alan O'Connor.

It's not unusual for a team to follow a pennant run with a disappointing year. Such was the case for Sacramento in 1943, which saw the club go "first to worst" in an unmitigated disaster of a season. The Solons' misfortunes started before the team had even taken the field for spring training. After all, it was the second full year of the United States' involvement in World War II, with the tide turning in favor of the Allied Forces and a resultant expanded draft.

Just as the war effort sapped MLB clubs of prime talent (including megastars like Ted Williams and Bob Feller), an even greater effect was felt in the minor leagues. In 1941, the year the U.S. entered the war, there were 41 minor leagues in baseball. By the time the 1943 season started, that number was whittled down to just nine.

Consequently, the Cardinals' usually replete farm system was thinned out, which meant there was precious little new personnel for Sacramento. So dire was the situation that St. Louis ran an advertisement in the *Sporting*

News that bluntly stated, "Cardinal Organization Needs Players." "If you are a free agent and have previous experience, we may be able to place you to your advantage on one of our clubs," read one desperate line, urging anyone willing and able to apply immediately. That MLB's defending World Series champions had to run a standard want ad was an apt measure of the impact the draft had on the entire sport.

When the season commenced, the Solons sported only four members of the 1942 pennant-winning squad. Many of the heroes from the prior year had enlisted, including Tony Freitas, Tommy Thompson, Frank Nelson, and Bill Endicott. Others, like Ray Mueller and Eddie Lake, were scooped up by major league clubs.

Pepper Martin, whose hard-nosed style galvanized the '41 and '42 teams, opted not to return as manager. His replacement was Ken Penner, a near-career minor league pitcher whose two years of MLB action were a far cry from Martin's St. Louis heroics. Worse, the roster was mostly made up of inexperienced players in a way that recalled "Killefer's Kiddies" in 1936.

With their pennant-winning core temporarily decimated, the *Madera Tribune* predicted a "riches to rags" season in 1943 for the Solons. The sentiment was shared by club president Phil Bartelme himself, who summed up their hopes for a repeat in three words: "Not a chance."

The war not only affected the team's makeup, but also its usually abundant fan support. The fate of the world was, after all, a higher priority than baseball, and Sacramentans were either consumed by following its every development or working tirelessly in industry to supply the Armed Forces. Government-mandated energy and gasoline restrictions had a severe impact too, eliminating night games and forcing many fans to take the trolley to Cardinal Field.

At season's end, only 31,600 would pass through the gates at Solons home games. Yet while the restrictions of wartime played a significant part, fans were no doubt driven away just as much by the club's historic futility. Sacramento failed to win a single series all season, en route to a 41-114 record, the worst in Pacific Coast League history. The offense only generated 424 runs (352 less than league champion Los Angeles), and their bumbling defense notched 239 errors. This adversely affected the pitching staff, which sported three 20-game losers.

Saving graces were scarce. The only pitcher worthy of praise, Al Brazle, led the PCL in ERA (1.69) and pitched 40 consecutive scoreless innings. But he was called up by the Cardinals in July as they headed to the World Series for the second year in a row. Fresh-faced 17-year-old Vernal "Nippy" Jones led the team in batting average and doubles, the first of many memorable years that would make him one of the most beloved ballplayers in Sacramento history later on.

Solons fans likely couldn't imagine things getting any worse than they were in 1943. But the following year brought back a frightening possibility worse than any last-place finish: the team leaving Sacramento. After Branch Rickey departed the Cardinals for the Brooklyn Dodgers in October 1942, St. Louis's bond with the Solons became a tenuous one. In February of 1944, it was reported they were ready to sell Sacramento to new ownership.

Almost immediately, Tacoma moved to buy the franchise. The Sacramento Chamber of Commerce sprang into action in a last-ditch effort to prevent the move, encouraging other PCL owners to oppose relocation. Cardinals president Sam Breadon offered the team for a $110,000 price tag, which included Cardinal Field.

With only two days left until Tacoma's acquisition would become official, *Sacramento Union* sports editor Dick Edmonds and his nightclub owner friend Yubi Separovich miraculously came up with $60,000 (enough to cover the cost of the team) and hopped on a train towards Southern California. Sportswriter James Lindsley would later aptly capture the improbability of the two being the ones to save the team, describing Edmonds as a "sports editor who is a self-confessed umpire-baiter" and "prone to howl like a wolf when one of the blue-coated arbiters gets so much as a sixteenth of an inch out of line."

Unlikely saviors as they were, they were men on a mission to get the money to PCL president Clarence Rowland and other owners before the Tacoma sale was finalized. They would have to persevere against nature itself, as a massive snowstorm halted their train 100 miles outside L.A. They improvised and managed to get on a bus, but that too was slowed down by heavy flooding.

By the time they arrived at the meeting, it was three hours late, and Rowland informed them the sale to Tacoma was set in stone. Edmonds and Separovich proffered their checks for $60,000, and Rowland urged the other owners to let them make their case for keeping the Solons in the River City. The owners were moved by their passion and voted unanimously to prevent the move. President Charles Graham of the San Francisco Seals and C.L. Laws of the Oakland Oaks were particularly crucial in voicing their opposition to the sale.

It was the closest the franchise had come yet to being moved, but they survived by the skin of their teeth thanks to the resolve of Sacramento fans. A group of Sacramento businessmen banded together to share ownership duties. They included Joe O'Neil as president, Roy Deary as vice president, Harry Ludwig filling the role of secretary, and George Klumpp, Vincent Stanich, E.L. French, and Dr. Alfred Oliver serving as assistant directors. Separovich was appointed general manager, a culmination of years of devotion to the team that began in his younger days proffering peanuts and programs at Moreing Field.

It would only be apropos that the Solons reward the efforts of the fans and businessmen who saved them with a good season, especially after the embarrassment of 1943. To effectively signify a fresh start, the stadium was once again renamed via a newspaper contest and was now called Doubleday Park. Former 1928 Senators star Earl Sheely, now working as a Red Sox scout, was tapped to be the manager.

The 1944 Solons wouldn't end up as incompetent as the prior year's team. But that was only because the 1943 iteration was historically awful. This team wasn't exactly a stirring improvement, finishing second to last at 76-93. The roster was mostly young and inexperienced, and it showed primarily in their league-worst .248 team average. Fortunately, more disappointing play didn't affect attendance, which soared to near 200,000 for the entire season.

However, trouble was stirring behind the scenes with the new front office. In a contentious stockholders' meeting in November, only Ludwig and Klumpp were kept, while the rest were replaced by newcomers Ed Wright, Louis Vienna, and Rod Weckworth. Separovich joined the board as well and handed over general manager duties to Earl Sheely.

When the calendar flipped to 1945, that insular turmoil ballooned into a full-blown scandal. Harry Ludwig quickly found himself in the crosshairs of

Leslie O'Connor, who was acting as temporary MLB Commissioner after the death of Kenesaw Mountain Landis. O'Connor was suspicious of Ludwig's business interests, one of which, the Lafayette Grill on K Street, was a hotbed of gambling. Given how resolute the late "Judge" Landis was in banning the 1919 Black Sox for throwing the World Series, O'Connor no doubt sought to follow in his footsteps by cracking down on any semblance of gambling within the realm of professional baseball.

Surprisingly, Ludwig opted not to defend his name and resigned accordingly. His shares were divvied up amongst Separovich, Frank Radich and Ed Sparks, all three of them figures in the liquor business. George Klumpp, who would soon be elected mayor of Sacramento, was chosen as team president.

More importantly, Sheely assembled a much ampler roster than the largely inept, untested ones that stumbled through 1943 and 1944. The most important pickup was Joyner "Jo-Jo" White, who helped the Detroit Tigers win their first World Series in 1935 and was still a brilliant baserunner. Sheely traded two players to acquire outfielder Jesse Landrum, with pitcher Joe Wood Jr., third baseman Jimmy Grant and catcher Norm Schlueter also arriving via trade.

The team got off to a lethargic start, sitting at fifth place through May. The biggest headlines came from a rumor started by popular Hollywood gossip columnist Louella Parsons. According to her, actress Betty Grable and her husband Harry James wanted to buy the Sacramento franchise. Whether it was true or not, such a move never materialized, and the Solons eventually crept up the standings.

Meanwhile, attendance remained consistently good, topping 233,000 for the first time since 1928. Fans were primarily enthralled by Sacramento's muscular offense, led by Jo-Jo White's .355 batting average. The Solons were also defensively brilliant, leading the PCL in fielding percentage with .968. Pitching was their biggest weakness, although Guy Fletcher won an impressive 24 games.

Just like in 1935 and 1942, 1945 brought another heartbreaking death near and dear to the team. *Union* sports editor Dick Edmonds, who had helped save the team just one year prior, died on July 19 from viral pneumonia at age 31, and was buried at the cemetery across Riverside Boulevard right by the Solons stadium. Fittingly, fans launched a campaign to rechristen the stadium in his honor. The ownership acquiesced and renamed Doubleday Park as Edmonds Field in September.

With 95 wins, Sacramento finished third and qualified for the post-season. They dispatched Seattle in the first round to face the fourth-place San Francisco Seals next. San Francisco took the first three games, but Sacramento managed to roar back with three to force a seventh game. They looked like they would complete the comeback from down three-games-to-none with a four-run lead, but the Seals staged a comeback to win 9-6.

Despite coming up short in the Governor's Cup, good news arrived soon thereafter. The club entered a working agreement to provide players to a farm team in Wenatchee, WA in the Western International League. Best of all, World War II finally ended in August, meaning thousands of baseball players would be returning eager to play once again.

The world of minor league baseball was quickly restored to its former breadth. The total number of minor leagues jumped practically overnight from 12 in 1945 to 43 in 1946. The Solons would field a record 55 players in 1946, hoping that offering as many contracts as possible would net them an optimal roster. Old favorites like Tony Freitas, Tommy Thompson and Gene Lillard were back, along with ex-major leaguers like Joe Marty and Al Smith.

While it was sentimental to open the door to so many old players and war veterans looking for a new start, it wasn't exactly conducive to assembling a championship team. The hitting was sluggish, hardly surprising given almost the entire starting lineup was in their mid-to-late thirties. Despite improved play as the season progressed, the Solons slipped in August and early September, finishing fifth and missing the playoffs.

Yet this hardly mattered to Sacramento fans, who turned out like never before all season long. With the specter of war and its ensuing labor requirements in their rearview mirror, a record 349,900 patrons passed through the turnstiles, the highest in Sacramento baseball history. PCL attendance as a whole tallied an incredible 3.7 million for the year.

Even with the healthy profits of higher attendance, the infighting amongst shareholders continued once again. Sheely and Separovich split in their vision of whose respective faction should own the most of the team's 2,500 shares. President George Klumpp tried to intervene and take control. The warring factions eventually agreed to a compromise that divvied up the shares relatively diplomatically. This new lineup fired Sheely, who accepted it rather amiably. Granted, it helped that the ownership paid him the remaining $20,000 on his contract.

With the ownership rancor seemingly settled, it was time to find a new manager for the 1947 season. They opted for Dick Bartell, a former All-Star MLB shortstop and coach of great renown. Bartell was a tough, salty character, one who could ostensibly whip an underachieving team into shape.

As it turned out, Bartell's approach crossed the line from tough to downright overbearing. The team wasn't exactly a contender to begin with, chiefly because their pitching staff was constantly being shuffled and had no stability as a result (they fielded 23 pitchers total). But the Solons' on-field play was largely overshadowed by Bartell's truculence.

For starters, rumors quickly circulated that he was at odds with various players, Freitas among them. Some reports said he fined players for missing signals. Another claimed he injured outfielder John Rizzo in a fistfight. Bartell denied all of these claims, but on none other than July 4, his rage boiled over when he got into a brawl with San Diego pitcher (and former Sacramento player) Tom Seats. Unsurprisingly, the Solons finished second above last at 83-103.

Once the season ended, many shareholders wanted to pay Bartell enough to release him in favor of a new manager. Reports persisted that several players wouldn't return if Bartell was manning the dugout in 1948. In mid-November, Chicago attorney Oscar Salenger bought half of the team's 2,500 shares. Much like John I. Taylor and Lew Moreing long ago, an ambitious new figure had control of the team, and promised to do everything in his power to make them a winner once again.

The first step was to make the team young again. Sacramento's recent rosters had relied too much on trying to win in the short term with old veterans, rather than develop new young talent for the long run. Salenger also fired Bartell, to the delight of many.

The retooling didn't work at all, as Sacramento plummeted to dead last in 1948. But that was far from their biggest concern that year. On July 11, several embers quickly turned into an inferno that destroyed Edmonds Field in its entirety, save for a section of the covered bleachers in left field and the outfield fence and light poles. But the grandstand, bleachers, dressing rooms and offices were an ashen heap, at a loss of $1,000,000 total.

The infamous fire of 1948 that destroyed Edmonds Field, and the Solons' season as a result. Photo courtesy of Alan O'Connor.

In one instant, decades of comfort and history had been incinerated. In the present, the fire had a two-fold impact. First, it forced the Solons to play the rest of the season on the road. Second, the ownership troubles ever present since the Cardinals era ended intensified. Salenger wanted to contract an outside company to provide concessions, even though Separovich pointed out the team already made most of its revenue providing their own concessions.

Later, Separovich told the rest of the board that Salenger had never paid him the $90,000 he owed for 600 shares. After the fire, both Salenger and Separovich settled things by selling all of their shares to a new group led by Klumpp, Ed Sparks, Harry Devine and Victor "Cookie" Devincenzi (a former owner of the Oakland Oaks). With so much turmoil and no home games for half the year, it was easy to overlook how alarmingly bad the team itself was. New manager Joe Orengo didn't adhere to Salenger's wishes for young talent, instead recruiting veterans like 39-going-on-40 future Hall of Famer Ernie Lombardi at catcher.

Needless to say, everything needed an overhaul before the 1949 season. First was a new stadium, a state-of-the-art concrete facility built at the same spot at Riverside and Broadway which was named Edmonds Field once again. The new ownership and front office were made official, and Del Baker, who had managed the Detroit Tigers to the World Series in 1940, was tapped as skipper. Former Sacramento Senator and Brooklyn Dodgers National League MVP Dolph Camilli also came aboard as a coach.

By every measure, 1949 was a refreshing success for the team after the tribulation of 1948. They obliterated their all-time attendance record, with 447,500 pouring into the stands to relish the new iteration of Edmonds Field. The team kept rising in the standings throughout the summer, keyed by Joe Marty's .327 average, while the offense as a whole hit and stole bases excellently. At 102-85, they finished third and made the playoffs, although they were quickly brushed aside by Hollywood.

Little did Sacramento baseball fans know it'd be the last taste of success they would enjoy for a long, long time.

Edmonds Field in 1949 after its rebuilding. Photo courtesy of Alan O'Connor.

SEVEN

LOSING STREAK: THE 1950S

No one could have known it from the outset, but the '50s would turn out to be a dreadful decade for the Solons and their fans. At the dawn of 1950, things didn't seem to be heading in that direction. Sacramento had a winning season the previous year, broke their all-time attendance record, and struck a working agreement with the Chicago White Sox. It was the first time they would be an affiliate club since serving in the Cardinals' farm system, when they enjoyed their greatest success.

1950, however, offered little to savor. The team stumbled into seventh through May, then disappeared into last place for the remainder of the year. Amidst the slog of a disappointing season, the Solons and their fans enjoyed a sentimental moment in May after 42-year-old Tony Freitas was released to make room on the roster. While a routine transaction, it marked the end of a rich career in the capital city that stretched back to 1929. Freitas had thrilled thousands of fans with many a gem on the pitcher's mound, most indelibly the ones he threw in the final games of 1942 to secure the PCL pennant.

Fans were better off relishing those memories than focusing on the Solons' increasingly miserable campaign in 1950. Just a week after the Freitas retirement ceremony, manager Red Kress and coach Lindsay Brown were dismissed. Fan favorite Joe Marty filled the spot at the managerial helm, but he was faced with the task of rescuing the team from last place despite having no previous managerial experience. The team did play a bit better under his leadership, but not enough to escape the cellar.

While finishing last, the club did reach a noble milestone on August 24 when it signed its first African American players, second baseman Marvin Williams and pitcher Walt McCoy. Coming three years after Jackie Robinson broke the major league color barrier with the Brooklyn Dodgers, the Solons were perfectly in step with the growth of black players in pro baseball; in fact, they integrated long before several major league clubs did. They couldn't lay claim to being integration pioneers in the PCL, though, as San Diego had featured the league's first black player, Johnny Ritchey, two years prior.

After record-setting attendance in 1949, the Solons saw a significant decline at the gates. Poor play alone wasn't to blame; the Korean War commenced in June, resulting in a draft that syphoned players from baseball (albeit not on the scale that World War II did). A new entertainment source, the television, was finding its way into households across the nation. As was often the case during a losing stretch, another new ownership committee, led by Eddie Mulligan, took over in October.

1951 looked like it was poised to be a turnaround season. Marty was replaced at manager with Joe Gordon, who had just finished his esteemed major league career and would also man second base for the team. At mid-June, Sacramento resided in first place with a 44-33 record, thanks largely to Gordon's exceptional hitting and fielding.

The rest of the team simply wasn't up to par with the future Hall of Famer. First baseman Bob Boyd and catcher Vinnie Smith hit consistently, but no one else did in the second half. The outfield, featuring Marty, Ralph Hodgin, Al White, and Herm Reich, were all well into their thirties, and their hitting declined as the season wore on. What started as an exhilarating first place run fizzled out into a 75-92, seventh place disappointment. Another blow came when the White Sox didn't renew their working agreement, depriving the Solons of a crucial pipeline for new personnel.

The 1952 season wouldn't remedy Sacramento's baseball ills. Rather, it only worsened them. The Solons offense was historically dismal, their .241 team average being the franchise's lowest since the disastrous 1910 Senators (whose .203 mark set a PCL record). Even Gordon was part of the problem, hitting just .246 and benching himself on several occasions. They finished last at an abysmal 66-114.

The remainder of the '50s proved much the same. In past decades, the franchise went through their share of peaks and valleys from year to year, normal for any professional ballclub. But this decade offered no respite, with only a single winning record and not one playoff appearance.

There were a few highlights. The most popular player of the era was Nippy Jones, who started with the '40s teams in his youth. Jones hit consistently well for Sacramento, later winning a World Series with the Milwaukee Braves in 1957. Ray Dandridge, a former Negro Leagues legend and future Hall of Famer, briefly played for the 1953 team. The 1956 team finished at .500 thanks to an impressive roster that boasted Jones, future Red Sox manager and Sacramento native John McNamara, Christian Brothers High School graduate and former MLB All-Star Wally Westlake, and 1948 Cleveland Indians World Series pitching hero Gene Bearden.

The dirge of the early '50s teams was also occasionally alleviated by the antics of pitcher "Chesty" Chet Johnson, who had many unique gags that made fans laugh as much as cheer. He loved to do a double-windmill windup and would often whip out a little black book to "consult" when a batter stepped up to the plate. If that batter got a hit, he would tear out a page in frustration.

Other times, he'd have the catcher throw the ball back to him so hard he'd pretend to fall over in agony. When players gathered around to see if he was hurt, he pulled off his glove to reveal a fake rubber thumb dripping blood. On other occasions, he sported a Davy Crockett coonskin cap as he took the field. Sacramento's otherwise scant attendance increased substantially every time he took the mound.

Yet no combination of players (or comic shenanigans), whether by acquiring veterans or trying out young local players, lifted the Solons out of the cellar. Not even bringing Tony Freitas aboard as manager could imbue them with a winning spirit. Once again, new ownership tried to right the ship in the middle of the decade. In November of 1954, the team avoided moving to Vancouver, but were still experiencing financial losses so tremendous that much of the ownership wanted out. On Christmas Eve, minority shareholder Fred David bought 632 stock certificates, thus becoming majority owner.

Tony Freitas as Solons manager in 1954. Despite many regal years on the pitcher's mound, he wasn't able to weave a similar magic for Sacramento as skipper. Photo courtesy of Alan O'Connor.

David was confident he had the answers to the team's manifold problems, and that they would stay in Sacramento "until hell freezes over." Given his long track record in local business, he had reason to believe he was capable of doing just that. Starting with his father's vegetable business at the

Sacramento Public Market at 12th and J Streets in his youth, David navigated a variety of professions before opening a restaurant and candy business that flourished in Sacramento in the '40s. His majority ownership also marked the culmination of a lifetime attachment to the franchise, going back to his youth in the '20s when he sold newspapers to players who congregated at a cigar store.

Owner Fred David (left) being interviewed by a sportscaster on local TV Channel 40 about the upcoming 1955 season. Photo courtesy of Alan O'Connor.

Sadly, the 1955 team offered no indication for any such optimism, with another last place finish and attendance around 22,600 below 1954's total. David was quickly in a tough financial situation, needing to pay off a $25,000 loan from the PCL in addition to covering losses from the meager fan support. Not even an influx of cash from a deal with the Chicago Cubs erased their debt issues, although it did enable them to at least keep operating.

A scorebook from the 1956 season, complete with the team's classic logo of the ebullient Solon dome sliding into second. Photo courtesy of Alan O'Connor.

After a much more respectable 84-84 record in 1956, one would hope it meant a step in the right direction after so many losing years. The club and fans entered the 1957 season with great expectations, and the players even sported brand new uniforms that proudly displayed "SOLONS" in red lettering. But they couldn't build on the previous year's promise, losing 14 of their first 18 games en route to a seventh-place finish. The fans, hopeful at the season's opening, showed up in the smallest amount in 15 seasons.

The 1956 Solons, whose .500 record was one of the few respectable campaigns of the entire decade. Notable players on this team included Nippy Jones (top row, left), Gene Bearden (top row, second from right), Wally Westlake (middle row, fourth from left), and John McNamara (middle row, third from right).

EIGHT

THE FINAL OUT: THE END OF THE SOLONS

As if years of losing hadn't already put the Solons' future in a precarious position, 1958 would hasten their demise. It was the year Major League Baseball finally commenced operation in California, and San Francisco became the new home of one of its eminent franchises, the New York Giants. Alongside the Brooklyn Dodgers' move to Los Angeles, it was a momentous occasion for both the state and professional baseball. Yet for loyal Sacramento baseball fans, there was reason for concern that it would overshadow their struggling team. Giants ticket manager Pete Hoffman promised fans that the team "wouldn't bother [the Solons] at all."

Fred David would have none of it. After the two franchises were approved to come in May 1957, he decried it as an act of monopoly. "If it isn't a monopoly, what can you call it when a big-league team comes out here and puts us out of business?" he asked. "They not only would be taking our business away from us but also depriving us of a chance to recoup losses we have suffered in the past." He wasn't the only PCL executive who held this view. Seattle general manager Dewey Soriano threatened a $3 million indemnity lawsuit, while David demanded $1,700,000. Vancouver GM

Cedric Tallis and San Diego president James Mulvaney listed their damages at $1,000,000 each.

David's concerns proved valid. Despite Hoffman's assurance, the arrival of the Giants did indeed have an immediate, and sometimes direct, impact on the Solons' popularity. Both teams played at home on the same day 35 times in 1958. KFBK, which had broadcast Solons games since their first season of night baseball in 1930, dropped Sacramento in favor of airing Giants games both at home and on the road. Ticket sales tapered off significantly, as box seat and general admission sales were just half what they were in 1957.

Given the contrast in on-field product, one could hardly blame fans for making the trip to San Francisco or staying home to enjoy the radio or television broadcast instead. The Giants had won the World Series four years before and sported future Hall of Famers like vivacious outfielder Willie Mays and N.L. Rookie of the Year first baseman Orlando Cepeda. Additionally, future Hall of Fame first baseman Willie McCovey was in the minor league pipeline and would make his debut the following season.

The 1958 Solons simply didn't have any players to compete with the novelty of the Giants' star-studded lineup. Their roster was composed mostly of familiar faces. Nippy Jones, fresh off helping the Milwaukee Braves win the 1957 World Series, returned to play first base. Infielder Dick Cole was another familiar face, albeit his return was a full 15 years since he played for the Solons briefly in 1943. Harry Bright would patrol the infield once again. The outfield welcomed back the likes of Jim Greengrass, Jim Westlake and Al Heist once more. One telling sign was that the Solons would have to play the '58 season without one of their best players, pitcher Milo Candini... because of his retirement at age 41.

Fans likely would have turned out in greater numbers had the Solons' well-worn roster proved to be a winner. Instead, they continued the losing ways that defined the team throughout the '50s. At 71-83, they weren't last like many teams that decade, but still placed a listless sixth place in the PCL. They did rank dead last in total attendance, however, with a scant 95,200, only the second time since 1936 that a Sacramento team failed to pass the 100,000 mark. The nadir came in June when one Friday night game drew 1,200, far exceeded by the 9,500 who opted instead for the County

Fair. Meanwhile, the Giants entertained more than 1,000,000 fans at Seals Stadium in 1958, while finishing a strong 80-74.

The excitement over the Giants and paltry attendance at Edmonds Field worsened the Solons' financial troubles. The team had yawning debts to pay, most urgently a $250,000 loan from the city employee retirement system. The Sacramento Chamber of Commerce started a "Keep Baseball in Sacramento" committee to boost home attendance towards the end of the season, to no avail. Team president Fred David resorted to selling off players to major league teams, much like Lew Moreing and Earl McNeely long before him, but only a few of them were of any value. Multiple cities, chiefly Tacoma and Victoria, were inquiring about moving the team.

Desperate, David moved forward with a plan to sell Edmonds Field and lease it back from the buyer for two years. If there were no takers on his offer, he would likely have to sell the team instead. They had suffered another financial loss as a result of low ticket sales, this one to the tune of $113,000.

In January of 1959, the stakes became clearer. David asked for a loan from other PCL owners to keep them afloat for another season, but they refused. Just like in the past, the Sacramento Chamber of Commerce came through with a fundraising campaign that would buy the team, but not Edmonds Field. The drive proved successful, raising over $175,000 from 400 individuals to form a new shareholder group, Solons Inc. The Milwaukee Braves, who won the World Series recently in 1957 thanks to Sacramento talents Nippy Jones and Felix Mantilla, struck a working agreement that hoped to make the Solons contenders once again.

To say the least, the pressure was on the team to dramatically improve in 1959. Fan favorite Nippy Jones returned to first base for his final season in the River City, while Clay Dalrymple, Bob Roselli and Cuno Barragan comprised the depth at catcher. The pitching staff got a boost from Milwaukee when they sent Panamanian hurler Winston Brown, who went on to lead the staff in most categories that season.

Things started promisingly with a 26-14 record that put them in first place. Outfielder Al Heist reached a streak of 154 games without an error, breaking the PCL record. The team's success stretched into the summer, boosting attendance tremendously as a result and eclipsing their paltry

1958 total by the end of July. In August, however, the magic began to fade, and the Solons dropped to third place, eventually settling at fourth with a 78-76 record. On the upside, they had their first winning record since 1949 and higher fan support.

In 1960, however, the Solons returned to their losing ways with a sixth-place finish. More fans continued to follow the Giants and Major League Baseball instead. But there was tumult before players even took the field, as Solons Inc. fired their general manager, Bill Brenner, right before the season commenced. Brenner became a subject of scrutiny when PCL vice president Dewey Soriano made recommendations for the team's operations that weren't carried out. Soriano then told the board they shouldn't let Brenner acquire players without the approval of team president Bill Golsong.

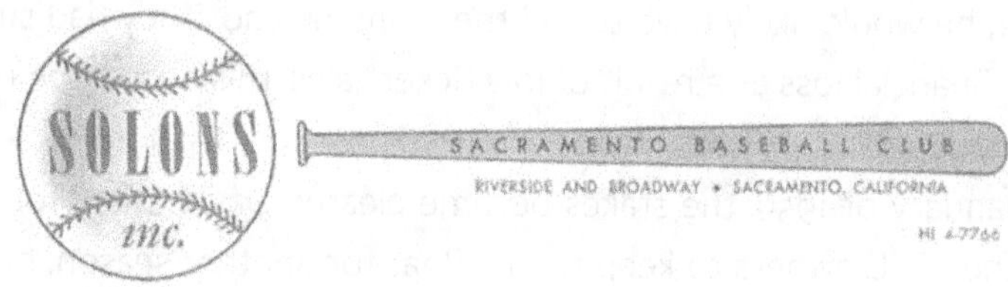

June 2, 1960

Dear Fellow Stockholder

The Board of Directors have designated Saturday, June 5, as Stockholders Nite at the local ball park.

To make this a successful evening and in recognition of the standing of the team it is their desire that you persuade or bring personally five of your close friends to the ball game. The Board feels sure that with a small amount of effort on your part together with the fine weather we are having will without a question make this a very successful evening.

May we again ask your complete cooperation.

Sincerely yours

SOLONS, INC.

W. B. Golsong
President

WBG/hd

A letter sent to Solons stockholders for a midseason event from team president William Golsong. Note the emphasis on bringing a substantial number of companions to the game, a reflection of the team's dire financial straits. Photo courtesy of Alan O'Connor.

Golsong proceeded to urge the Solons Inc. board to dismiss Brenner altogether, which they quickly did by a 5-3 vote. It turned out to be a necessary move, as Soriano uncovered many deals done by Brenner that he had kept in the dark from Golsong. It was an important matter to resolve quickly, but it ultimately made little difference given Sacramento's losing record that season. To make matters worse, attendance declined and Milwaukee ended their working agreement with the club.

Numerous times, the franchise faced the threat of moving out of Sacramento and managed to stave it off. But this time, the situation was beyond repair. PCL owners issued a deadline to the Solons brass: get the team's situation figured out by November 15 or lose it. They had suffered another loss of $100,000 and had a scant number of players to sell to raise money.

The Solons Inc. board went to work again, this time not to fire a general manager, but to determine the fate of the entire franchise. They came to a 4-4 vote on two measures: one to dissolve Solons Inc., the other to continue team operations by raising money via a ticket drive. After a second vote, they went forward with the ticket drive, but it was unsuccessful. They hoped to sell 100,000 tickets in advance for free access to games in 1961, but ended up with only 4,400 takers.

At long last, the end came. The board quickly voted 7-0 to dissolve the team and sell it. There was one last attempt at a ticket drive on October 19 that fell short. Once the mid-November deadline arrived, the team was put up for sale. The PCL purchased the Solons, as many directors insisted that they buy the club due to its inability to meets its final obligations to the league. The league then sold the franchise to two Salt Lake City executives, who moved them to Hawaii.

For decades, the Senators and Solons franchise played for record crowds and paltry ones. They fielded a bevy of future and former major league stars, as well as cherished local favorites. Despite many finishes in the cellar, they won two consecutive President's Cups in the '30s and a miraculous PCL pennant in 1942. They were the team that introduced the rest of the league to the magic of night baseball.

They survived the ebbs in popularity wrought by the Great Depression and World War II, to the point where it seemed nothing could end them.

Not even Edmonds Field going up in flames had forced them to leave Sacramento. Now, however, it all came to an official end with the mere stroke of a pen. Golsong signed the sale papers on January 4, 1961, and the Solons were off to Honolulu, Hawaii to become the Islanders.

In the months following the Solons' January move, 1961 marked the beginning of the expansion era in Major League Baseball. California welcomed its third franchise, the Los Angeles Angels. The Washington Senators, who won their lone World Series in 1924 thanks to Sacramento's Earl McNeely, moved to Minnesota to become the Twins. A new Washington franchise, also called the Senators, took their place (although they too would eventually move to Texas and become the present-day Rangers). 1962 witnessed the additions of the New York Mets and the Houston Colt .45s (later the Astros).

Yet the sudden frenzy of expansion wouldn't find its way to Sacramento. After a century of pioneering baseball in the Golden State, the city painfully said goodbye to its professional team just as major league clubs began taking the field in nearby major cities. It was a void that would ultimately take many years to fill.

NINE

A GIANT FAREWELL: MAJOR LEAGUE BASEBALL SENDS OFF EDMONDS FIELD

The departure of the Solons was a devastating blow for local fans, who were left without professional baseball for the first time since World War I. No teams, minor or major league, came to town in the immediate aftermath of the 1961 move. Edmonds Field remained comfortably nestled on Broadway, albeit not for long.

The property was eventually sold to Lucky Stores Inc., who would demolish it in May of 1964. But in April of that year, the house that Edward Kripp built came alive one last time. As MLB's Cactus League spring training was winding down, the Cleveland Indians and San Francisco Giants rolled into town for two exhibition games before the regular season commenced a few days later.

Although in different leagues, the teams nonetheless shared an indelible historical link, having met ten years before in the 1954 World Series. This was when the Giants still took to the Polo Grounds of New York, entering the series as heavy underdogs. The Indians stormed their way to a then-American League record 111 wins with the dazzling pitching of Bob Feller, Bob

Lemon, Early Wynn, and Mike Garcia. In a best-of-seven series, beating a team with such a staff seemed like an insurmountable task.

With the first game in New York tied in the eighth inning, the Giants were galvanized by a highlight reel catch for the ages. With two runners on base, Indians slugger Vic Wertz launched a shot into the Polo Grounds' abnormally deep centerfield that seemed guaranteed to score two runs. But Giants centerfielder Willie Mays sprinted to keep up with it, making an improbable over-the-shoulder catch and spinning around to fire the ball back to the infield. Forever enshrined in baseball lore simply as "The Catch," it was all the Giants needed as they won the game on a walk-off home run and proceeded to sweep Cleveland for the championship.

The 1964 Cactus League games were, to say the least, nowhere near as important. Being exhibition games, they didn't carry the weight of a regular season matchup, let alone the high stakes drama of the Fall Classic. But that didn't make them any less exciting for baseball-starved Sacramentans.

For tickets merely priced at $3.50, $3 and $2, fans from the city and the Central Valley flocked to see major league stars like Mays, Willie McCovey, Orlando Cepeda, Matty Alou, Vic Davalillo, and Dick Howser roam Edmonds Field. The Indians' roster even featured a direct connection to the River City in infielder Woodie Held. The Sacramento native, who held the record for most homers by a Cleveland shortstop at the time, graced the cover of the official souvenir program.

The official souvenir program for the April 1964 exhibition games between the Giants and Indians, the last games played at Edmonds Field. Sacramento native Woodie Held proudly adorned the cover. Photo courtesy of Alan O'Connor.

The first contest on April 11 was a highly entertaining slugfest. Program cover boy Held fittingly blasted a home run, but the Giants had even greater power from Willie McCovey, who laced a home run of his own and 4 RBIs to lead San Francisco to a 12-7 victory. Willie Mays added to the onslaught with a double. The next day saw a slightly lower score, but a similar display of power from San Francisco's vaunted Mays-McCovey tandem. The duo launched back-to-back home runs over the left field scoreboard, keying a 7-6 Giants victory.

Hall of Fame Giants outfielder Willie Mays, regularly considered the greatest five-tool player of all-time, takes a swing during one of the last ever games at Edmonds Field in 1964. Photo courtesy of Alan O'Connor.

More significant than the final scores or mammoth hits of these games, however, was the somber reality that they were the last moments of baseball ever enjoyed at the confines of Edmonds Field. Once the Giants and Indians completed their second game on April 12, the only swings Edmonds Field had left to anticipate weren't those of Mays and McCovey, but the destructive blasts of steel wrecking balls. Beginning on May 1, the Sacramento landmark was demolished to make way for a Gemco discount store.

Today, the plot of land is the location of the Broadway/Riverside Target store. Fortunately, the succession of department stores hasn't erased all remembrance of the treasured baseball history that transpired there. Inside the front exit of Target, gracing the otherwise unadorned red wall, is a plaque commemorating the legacy of Edmonds Field.

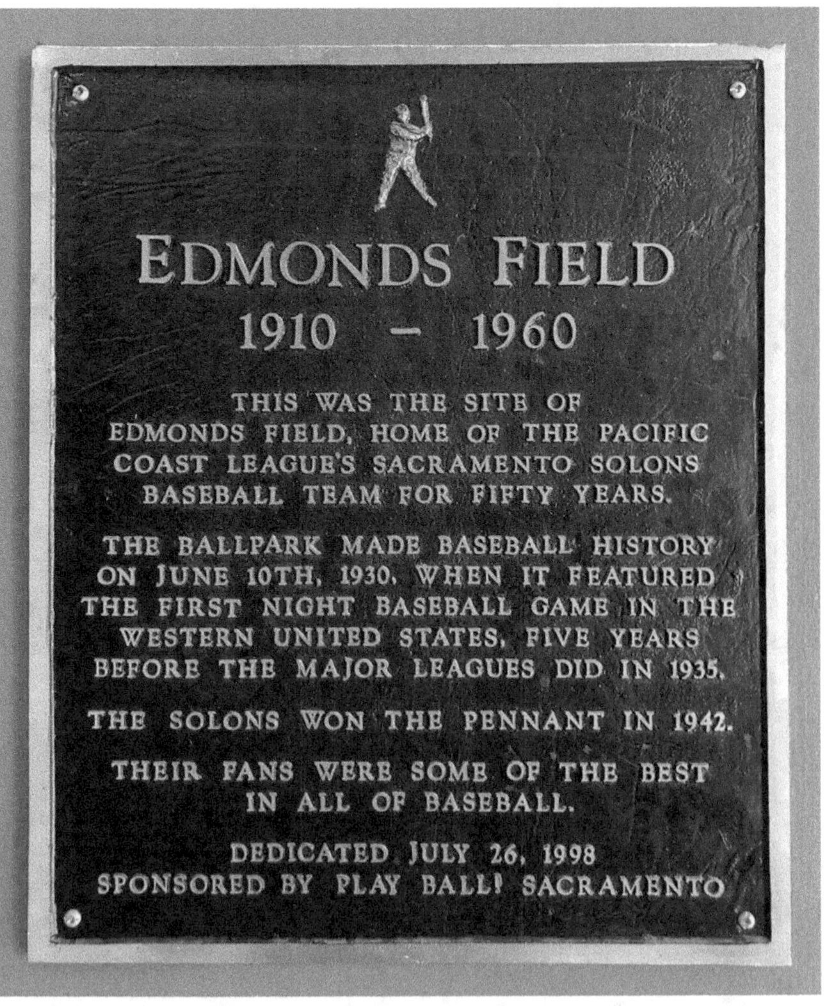

The commemorative plaque inside the Target on Riverside and Broadway honoring Edmonds Field. Photo taken by Morgan Garvey.

TARGET

The area on Riverside and Broadway as it looks today. The far corner of the parking lot is close to centerfield. Photos taken by Morgan Garvey.

TEN

1974-1976: BASEBALL (BRIEFLY) COMES HOME

By the mid-1970s, professional baseball in Sacramento was almost a distant memory. Following the Solons' departure for Hawaii after 1960 and the demolition of Edmonds Field shortly thereafter, no team readily stepped in to fill the void like in the late 19th and early 20th centuries. It wasn't for lack of trying; Fred David, former team owner and a majority stockholder for the Edmonds Field property, lobbied Sacramento city and county to buy the treasured stadium and bring a new PCL club there. When that proposition failed, David and 80 other stockholders were at least able to split $850,000 from Lucky Stores Inc., who purchased the Broadway and Riverside property and demolished Edmonds Field to pave way for a Gemco store.

As it were, baseball would seem to be the farthest thing from the minds of most Sacramento citizens in the mid-'70s. The city underwent a series of tumultuous events and political shifts of both local and national significance. In October 1973, the Organization of Arab Petroleum Exporting Countries suddenly implemented an oil embargo in retaliation for U.S. support of Israel in the Yom Kippur War.

The price-per-barrel of oil quadrupled by the embargo's end in March 1974, leading to unprecedented fuel shortages and serpentine lines of cars waiting at gas stations across the country. In January 1975, upcoming Republican presidential contender Ronald Reagan was succeeded by Democrat Jerry Brown as California's governor.

Brown, in a manner befitting the prevailing trends of energy shortages and inflation, declared an "era of limits." After his father oversaw a prodigious boom in the '60s with ambitious expansions of infrastructure and higher education, the younger Brown focused instead on limiting spending and balanced budgets. It didn't help that he did his work in a dilapidated California statehouse, which was in such disrepair that it had a sign warning visitors to enter at their own risk. In September 1975, U.S. President Gerald Ford survived his second assassination attempt in less than a month when Manson Family cult member Lynette "Squeaky" Fromme's gun failed as he walked the Sacramento capitol grounds to a meeting with Brown.

The political unease and sickness of post-Watergate/Vietnam War America had come to Sacramento in near deadly fashion. The same year Ford was nearly gunned down at the capitol, a literal sickness hit the city when a Myalgic Encephalopathy/Chronic Fatigue Syndrome (ME/CFS) outbreak suddenly began in Carmichael, affecting some 200 people throughout the course of 1975.

Yet even with all of these trying developments, Sacramento remained a fertile ground for entertainment. An outsized number of the premiere rock and roll acts of the time played concerts at the Memorial Auditorium on J Street from 1974-76, among them Yes, Frank Zappa, The Eagles, Fleetwood Mac, and Blue Oyster Cult. On October 29, 1975, just two months after his breakthrough album *Born to Run* was released, Bruce Springsteen and his revamped E Street Band played a high-energy set as part of a tour that marked their rise as the biggest band in the world. In November 1976, Canadian progressive rock trio Rush performed the same year their respective breakthrough *2112* hit shelves. The American Freedom Train, a roving emblem of patriotic spirit meant to celebrate the nation's bicentennial, made a brief stop in Old Sacramento in November 1975 as part of its 48-state railroad tour.

These years also marked an eventful and transitory time for baseball across the nation. Atlanta Braves slugger Hank Aaron ascended to the sport's pinnacle of individual achievement when he hit his 715th career home run in April 1974, breaking Babe Ruth's record (albeit amidst a torrent of racist death threats). In 1973, the American League replaced the pitcher's spot in the batting order with the designated hitter, in hopes of generating more offense and fan interest after pitching dominated the '60s. Most importantly, the game's overall popularity, eclipsed by the professional football boom the prior decade, rebounded strongly thanks to the exhilarating 1975 World Series between the Cincinnati Reds and Boston Red Sox.

To say the least, it was an ideal period for baseball to return to Sacramento. In 1974, a full decade after the wrecking ball had reduced Edmonds Field to a pile of debris, the capital city would finally host a new Solons team. The word first broke in *The Sacramento Bee* in November 1973 that Bob Piccinini, a supermarket chain owner who also owned the California League's Modesto Reds club, was intent on moving the Pacific Coast League's Eugene Emeralds to Sacramento.

It was a process that had actually started on September 23, when general manager John Carbray reached out to various Sacramento officials about the idea, among them Dr. John Meyers of the Sacramento City Unified School District and Solon "Doc" Wisham of the City Recreation and Parks Department.

On December 1, PCL directors voted to approve the team's move to Sacramento. Carbray expressed deep gratitude: "Frankly, what's happening is unbelievable. I had checked out Las Vegas, Portland, Seattle, and Sacramento as sites, but I quickly realized this city contained more pluses than the other three." However, there were a few obstacles to overcome in order for Sacramento to reclaim its status as "the best baseball town of its size in the country," as *The Sporting News* christened it so many years ago.

The most challenging impediment to bringing in a new team was the lack of a stadium. The answer to this problem ultimately resided at the Sacramento City College campus, whose football field, Hughes Stadium, was hardly ideal. After all, its oval-shaped dimensions created a truncated left field that stood a mere 232 feet from home plate (with a 40-foot high screen on top of the wall to stifle excess home runs).

Sacramento Mayor Richard Marriott (fourth from left, wearing hat) presents Bob Piccinini (fourth from right, holding document) with a proclamation welcoming his franchise to Sacramento. Photo courtesy of the Sac City Express.

A far cry from Edmonds Field, where a ball hit 440 feet to centerfield could end up staying inside the park, the awkward dimensions at Hughes would make it an Eden for batters. Bob Lemon, the new Solons manager in their inaugural season, summed it up aptly: "Being a former pitcher I've always emphasized pitching and defense. Hughes Stadium could persuade me to change some of my strategy. We'll have some very exciting baseball with plenty of big innings. The last out will really count in this park."

Then there was the issue of getting to the stadium itself, as well as the lack of parking there. The OPEC embargo was still in full swing, keeping the U.S. in a severe gasoline shortage that made non-essential motor travel difficult. Carbray and the Sacramento Transit Authority thus devised a busing system that could transport anyone in the Sacramento metropolitan area to the game. It was a move that recalled the old Solons in the '40s, when World War II-induced gasoline rationing forced many fans to take trolleys to the stadium.

Carbray had the Los Rios Community College District lease 500 parking spaces at Hughes, with additional parking installed at Curtis Park and Sutterville Road. Even that wasn't without adversity, as some 1,300 students signed a petition protesting any baseball parking that would conflict with their night schedules. Their concerns weren't merely centered around convenience, as it would force more students to park at William Land Park and other adjacent areas that were considered unsafe after dark. Nonetheless, the night games and their required parking would continue unabated.

However, there was skepticism as to whether or not Sacramento fans would make all of this effort worthwhile. *Sac City Express* sportswriter Steve Connell noted the city's recent history of paltry attendance for major sporting events at Hughes Stadium. The first came in 1966, when the American Football League's Oakland Raiders and Denver Broncos played in front of just 15,000 (out of a capacity of 24,000). Especially given the geographical proximity of the Raiders and the AFL's highly popular emphasis on offense, the lack of a sellout was somewhat surprising.

In December 1973, an even more miniscule 12,016 came through the turnstiles to witness the annual Camellia Bowl. The college national football championship game had been played in Sacramento every year since 1961, but this Division II match between Louisiana Tech and Western Kentucky failed to generate an appropriate level of interest. William Golsong, the former president of the previous Solons franchise now serving as Camellia Bowl President, chastised fans for the paltry turnout.

Connell noted that many believed the Camellia Bowl was a test to see how much the city could support a new baseball team. As such, it seemed to indicate the second Solons would fail to fill the seats. Golsong, whose skepticism was likely exacerbated by the attendance issues that doomed the original Solons, observed: "There was a lot of promotion for this national championship game and we still didn't have a sellout. But if you're talking about a baseball team, I don't know...They're really going to have to sell it."

Nevertheless, with parking and transportation hurdles overcome, the Solons could finally get to business for the 1974 season. Officially becoming a minor league affiliate for the Milwaukee Brewers, Sacramento hired former Cleveland Indians pitcher Lemon as manager. This was two years before he was inducted into the Baseball Hall of Fame, and four before he managed the New York Yankees to a World Series title.

After training camp in Tempe, Arizona, the Solons poignantly began the regular season in Honolulu against their antecedent franchise, now known as the Hawaii Islanders. Hawaii won four out of a five-game series, but the Solons could leave with their heads high in anticipation of their first game at Hughes Stadium. It would be the first taste of professional baseball of any kind in Sacramento since the awesome power of Mays and McCovey sent off Edmonds Field a decade ago, and fans were ready to relish the moment.

Former City College student Glenn Wolff paints numbers on Hughes Stadium seats in preparation for the 1974 season. Photo courtesy of the Sac City Express.

The atmosphere of the home opener recalled the pomp and circumstance of the first PCL game at Oak Park in 1903, and in some ways exceeded it. The announced crowd of 17,318 was the largest baseball attendance in Sacramento history, and while players weren't shuttled to the stadium in a parade, the route there was accordingly packed with traffic due to the volume of fans. Highway 99 and the nearby turnoff onto the stadium's location on 12th Avenue was backed up, requiring police to direct traffic on the adjacent Freeport Boulevard. Mayor Richard Marriott threw out the first pitch, hearkening back to when Governor Pardee did the same at the PCL opener 71 years before.

The event wasn't without its hiccups. *Express* reporter Marty Stevenson lamented the "conspicuous absence" of beer as a concession, albeit admitting it "failed to darken the crowd's mood." More disappointing was a rip-off promotion where the public address announcer encouraged fans to look at a specific page in their programs to find a prize-winning lucky number. Such a number didn't exist, to the frustration of many fans.

Yet even underwhelming concessions and empty prize guarantees couldn't overshadow the poignant connections to Sacramento's baseball past that were in abundance. Former Solons player-manager Joe Gordon gave color commentary for local music and sports station KGMS, alongside broadcaster Roy Storey. Another connection came in an unlikely coincidence when Spokane Indians outfielder Don Castle hit the stadium's first home run. The ball cleared the left field screen, only to be caught in the stands by Carroll Canfield Jr., whose father Carroll Sr. pitched for the Sacramento Senators from 1921 to 1927.

To no one's surprise, the left field fence would define a team's hopes of victory on any given night. Spokane won the first game 10-3, then launched five homers in the next game for a 19-1 victory. In the third game, the Solons notched their first home victory with six round-trippers and 16 runs.

And so it went on, with double digit scores night after night. Hughes Stadium would witness only one shutout the entire year, a no-hitter by Spokane's Steve Dunning on August 16. The most awesome display of power came mere days later when the Solons launched nine homers in a game, setting the PCL record. These games may not have shown baseball at its purest and most strategic, but they certainly were entertaining. "You don't see anybody leaving early," noted Carbray. "Win or lose, it's exciting."

Opposing managers and pitchers groused about the field nonstop. It was "a Little League park with a big screen" in the words of Salt Lake City manager Norm Sherry, while Hawaii manager Roy Hartsfield was more profuse (and profane): "This is the worst (expletive) park in baseball. This place has put baseball back 100 years. You don't manage here, you just watch the sluggers perform. To hell with the sacrifice, the steal and the hit-and-run. I might just as well curl up in a corner and read a book."

One group who certainly had no qualms with Hughes Stadium were Solons fans, who made for a total attendance of 295,800 in 1974, the highest in the minor leagues in the U.S. that year. Golsong and Connell's skepticism of fan support had been proven resoundingly wrong, at least for the time being.

Even with the absurd advantage provided by Hughes Stadium's left field, the 1974 Solons boasted a lineup of truly excellent all-around players. Sacramento native and American River College alumnus Bill McNulty quickly became a fan favorite, blasting 55 home runs, the most of any player in the history of Sacramento pro baseball. He led the team in almost every single batting category, including average (.329), runs (135), hits (173), RBIs (135), and doubles (25). Outfielder Gorman Thomas was right behind him in home runs with 51, as both came close to Hall of Famer Tony Lazzeri's PCL record of 60 back in 1925. 20-year-old outfielder Sixto Lezcano cleared the fence 34 times himself, while also collecting a team-best eight triples. Outfielder Steve McCartney and designated hitter Tommie Reynolds both had 32 homers.

Of all the '70s Solons, Thomas went on to enjoy the greatest major league renown with the Brewers, most indelibly the 1982 squad. That season, his team-best 39 homers keyed the "Harvey's Wallbangers" offensive jugger-naut that slugged its way to the World Series. It was certainly a better end for Thomas than the '74 season finale, when he was benched by Carbray for poor behavior and lack of discipline throughout the year. "He's been purposely breaking bats and throwing helmets and using profane language within hearing and seeing distance of the crowd…I don't care how big a star he is. He's not ever going to play here again," fumed Carbray.

Even with record fan attendance, potent hitters and a copious amount of home runs, the Solons found themselves finishing last in the PCL. Their inflated home run total helped them to a 39-33 home record, which stood in stark contrast to a dismal 27-45 on the road. While the left field fence was heaven for Sacramento's offense, it was conversely hell on their pitching. Roger Miller's team-best ERA was an unsightly 4.48, while Tom King had the worst at 10.32. There was simply no avoiding how untenable Hughes Stadium was as a home for the Solons, and while many proposals for a new facility were made, nothing came to fruition.

Despite the team's poor play in '74 and no new stadium, hopes were high for 1975. Harry Bright, a Sacramento native and popular infielder for the '50s Solons, took over the managerial reigns from Lemon. The left field screen was extended in hopes of stymying the absurd amount of home runs, as well as the acrimony they generated amongst opposing teams.

Carbray sought to capitalize on fervent fan interest with a series of promotions and novelties. The most outlandish was having the players wear Bermuda shorts for some of the games, a long-forgotten stunt pulled by the Hollywood Stars in 1950. Somehow, the shorts made their way to the majors the next year when the Chicago White Sox briefly donned them.

Of course, tacky promotions and tinkering with the field's dimensions wouldn't mean much if they weren't backed up by a winning team. The Solons failed to deliver in that regard. When the calendar flipped to June, they sported a meager 18 wins against 41 losses, en route to another finish in the cellar. Their home run total dropped from 305 in 1974 to just 196, although their defense was a substantial improvement. Once again, the pitching was subpar, with the bullpen performing better than the starting rotation. When the season concluded, they lay in dead last with a 59-85 mark.

There was one relative bright spot at the midpoint of an otherwise atrocious season. On June 5, the Milwaukee Brewers came to Hughes Stadium for an exhibition game against the Solons. Hank Aaron, just over one year removed from breaking Babe Ruth's all-time home run record, blasted a home run in the top of the fourth so gigantic it left the stadium entirely.

However, the spirit of that exposition belied the difficult relationship between the two franchises. In 1975, the Solons learned just how hard it is to balance winning as a minor league team with the demands of being an MLB affiliate. This meant their best players could be called up to the majors at any given moment, which hit them from the outset when Lezcano and Thomas were promoted early on and would ultimately spend all of 1975 in Milwaukee. (Granted, Thomas's promotion was congruent with Carbray's season-ending declaration that he'd never play with the Solons again.) Those were far from the only players affected, as there would be only five players total who played 100 or more games for Sacramento that year.

In many cases, this would merely be business as usual for a AAA working agreement. Yet the rest of the PCL owners felt the Brewers were failing to ensure Sacramento had enough quality players, even to the point of violating their official working agreement with them. Led by PCL president Roy Jackson, they approached MLB Commissioner Bowie Kuhn and American League President Lee MacPhail to rectify the situation. An incensed Tony Siegle, Milwaukee's farm director, derided their criticisms and insisted that the Brewers and Solons were on mutually good terms.

The skepticism of PCL owners was vindicated in August, when Milwaukee suddenly dropped Sacramento from its farm system. Siegle cited the familiar scapegoat Hughes Stadium as the primary reason, claiming the adjustments needed to overcome its quirks stunted player development. While Siegle's criticisms of the field and the PCL owners' protests over Milwaukee's negligence were both warranted, Hughes Stadium was undoubtedly the more pressing issue the team faced. Additionally, they faced financial losses hovering around $71,000. Worse, Piccinini dropped a bombshell all too familiar to Sacramento fans in early 1976: if the city couldn't procure a new stadium by September, the team would be sold or moved.

To make matters worse, the furor over parking hadn't subsided for some. City College sociology professor Betty Ford (not to be confused with the First Lady of the same name) cited Solons night game parking as a danger for female students in light of recent efforts to curb sexual assault on campus. "When the Solons play at Hughes Stadium or evening events are held it makes things so much worse for women," she stated.

It was an all-too familiar scenario: a losing team, financial uncertainty, and the looming possibility of relocation. One key difference between this incarnation of the Solons and the previous one was when the old team endured the periodic threats of moving, they could usually take comfort in the reliability of Edmonds Field. The new Solons, however, were in this position in the first place largely *because* of their stadium. Hughes was, after all, only ever to be a temporary stop until a new ballpark could be built.

Despite this, every initiative to secure a new facility went nowhere. A committee formed in 1975 to advocate for a 15,000-seat complex that could host multiple sports. Funding for the complex was tethered to a ballot measure in November, which proposed increasing property taxes by up to 10 cents per $100 of assessed value. However, the text on the ballot didn't clearly state that the funds would be used for building a stadium, and the measure was shot down by over 17,000 votes.

Amidst uncertainty about their future, the Solons took the field once again in 1976. They could at least look forward to a more stable working agreement with the Texas Rangers, who provided a top-notch new manager in Rich Donnelly and a bevy of hitting prospects. After the ugly fallout with Milwaukee cast a pall over the '75 season, the new relationship with Texas proved to be just the boost Sacramento needed. They finished 71-72, just below .500, and even managed to hold second place in the PCL Western Division early in the season.

As always, the offense was muscular and the pitching subpar-to-atrocious. As a team, they led the Pacific Coast League in batting, home runs and hits, and boasted six .300 hitters. Left-handed outfielder Lew Beasley led the pack with an incredible .351 average, and even the lowest average in the starting lineup was a respectable .251. The pitching staff, on the other hand, led the league in home runs allowed, walks and ERA. Their most notable pitcher was Len Barker, who won 11 games and would later pitch a perfect game for the Cleveland Indians in 1981.

Another notable player was infielder Bump Wills, the son of famous '60s Los Angeles Dodgers base-stealing phenom Maury Wills. The 1962 National League MVP even came to watch his son play in early May. He wasn't the only big name in Sacramento that week, as First Lady Betty Ford made a stop the following day to campaign for her husband Gerald's re-election bid (months after his assassination attempt in the same city no less). The elder Wills returned on August 14 for Bump Wills Night, put together by the team to honor his outstanding performance that season that included leading the Solons in home runs (26) and RBIs (95).

A much better record and a crop of MLB-ready talent should have resulted in even greater attendance. But despite flirting with contention and their biggest win total yet, the Solons entertained far fewer fans than the past two seasons. Hal Wehmeier, who had taken over as GM for John Carbray at the end of 1975, continued his predecessor's inclination for promotions.

However, those failed to do the trick; Helmet Night, the first giveaway of the season, attracted a paltry 2,100 fans. The total attendance for 1976 was just 82,300. It was not only dead last in the PCL, but the worst in Sacramento baseball history since the old Solons' dismal 1943 campaign. Of course, that was partly because of the distraction and travel restrictions resultant of World War II.

Solons players during a festive session of catch in 1976, which would prove to the best season yet for the new incarnation of the team. Unfortunately, it was also their last. Photo courtesy of Alan O'Connor.

Attendance was merely the beginning of the Solons' problems. Bob Piccinini's September 1 deadline came and went without a new stadium secured. Worse, Hughes Stadium needed to undergo repairs from an earthquake, rendering it unavailable for the 1977 season. Sacramento could no longer rest on the embattled football field as a makeshift home, and absolutely needed a new park to call their own.

Even before the earthquake, one particular episode in May painfully illustrated the inherent limits of playing at Hughes. The outfield fence sustained damage after the Solons forgot to remove it for an afternoon junior high school track meet. When a City College crew assembled to take care of it, their inadequately sized forklift couldn't properly lift the fence, knocking it over and leaving it flat on the ground. The stadium scoreboard and goal posts were also damaged.

Wehmeier angrily decried the crew's error as "a malicious act," a charge bluntly repudiated by Public Relations Officer Lawrence Benke. Benke publicly stated that the Solons had ignored a contract that stipulated they were required to remove the fence as requested for any scheduled school event on the field. Any failure to do so forced the district to do the work, and for the Solons to reimburse any costs.

The team had been notified of the May 7 track meet but had neglected to remove the fence. As a result, the City College crew didn't have enough time to get the proper equipment, leading to the hasty removal and damage. It seemed like a relatively trivial issue, but Wehmeier and Benke continued to shift blame back and forth over it. While a compromise was eventually reached, it became all the more urgent for the Solons to find a home exclusively for themselves.

A solution was proposed in late September by Wehmeier, who eyed Harry Renfree Field in Del Paso Park as the new home for his team. Wehmeier pitched the idea to the Sacramento City Council, with the stadium's capacity increased from 800 to 2,000. When the council conducted an official study, they concluded the cost of Wehmeier's proposal would run as high as $529,000, far more than the Solons GM anticipated. Once again, the drumbeats for moving the team were restarted, albeit with a catch: this move would have a built-in plan to bring them back to Sacramento.

In stepped Joe Gagliardi, the owner of the San Jose Bees in the California League. His initial idea earlier in the year was to move the Solons to San Jose, while his club moved to Sacramento in exchange. Now he sought to buy the Solons outright and move them to San Jose, without the quid pro quo of sending the Bees to Sacramento. PCL owners settled the matter in a nine-hour meeting in October, ruling that Gagliardi could not buy the team wholesale. However, the Solons were still allowed to move to San Jose until a new stadium was built in Sacramento. Gagliardi agreed to the terms, with a lease of up to three years.

Sadly, it would be a promise unfulfilled. The Solons franchise, now rechristened the San Jose Missions, failed to make waves in their new home. The Bay Area already had two MLB teams, the San Francisco Giants and Oakland Athletics, making the Missions a far less tantalizing attraction for San Jose fans than they might have been before. Although they were a minor league affiliate for Oakland, one of the winningest teams of the decade, they slogged to a dead last finish in 1977 in front of microscopic crowds.

After their win and attendance totals dropped even further in 1978, Bob Piccinini announced he had someone in line to buy the club and return them to Sacramento for the 1979 season. Nothing could be further from the truth. Not only did the team have debts on the order of $120,000, but in their absence, there was still no new facility built in Sacramento, meaning they'd once again have to settle for the awkward confines of Hughes Stadium. No major league team would seriously consider them as an affiliate in those circumstances. Instead, they were moved to the small city of Ogden, Utah.

Sacramento now had the ignominy of being the nation's largest city without professional baseball. Ideas came and went, from expanding the size of Hornet Field at Sacramento State to building a new baseball field at Cal Expo. The most notable effort came from developer Gregg Lukenbill, who built Arco Arena for the NBA's Sacramento Kings. In 1988, Lukenbill signed a deal to finance a state-of-the-art, 40,000-seat baseball stadium near Arco Arena. But five years later, the stadium remained unfinished during a time when Major League Baseball added two new expansion franchises (which ended up going to Denver, Colorado and Miami, Florida).

All told, Sacramento baseball fans would have to wait two-and-a-half decades for a team. The wait would be worth it, though, as the dawn of the new millennium brought Sacramento its most perennially successful franchise yet.

ELEVEN

SAFE AT HOME: THE ARRIVAL AND PERENNIAL SUCCESS OF THE RIVER CATS

For any sports franchise, winning consistently in a crowded league is an imperative and often elusive goal. There are indeed other measures of success for a team, such as individual performances and feats by players, or maintaining regular fan attendance and loyalty. As the seasons go on, however, the number of winning seasons, playoff appearances, and championships a franchise attains is of paramount importance. In baseball, for every team like the Yankees or Cardinals that can savor decades of winning, there are clubs like the Mariners and Padres who might just hope to make the playoffs in a given year.

Playing in the AAA level of the minor leagues, the Sacramento River Cats have been able to become a consistent winner on the field in less than two decades of existence, while meeting the constant demands of providing talent for a major league team. How did they come to distinguish themselves not only in over 150 years of Sacramento baseball history, but in the highest level of minor league baseball as well?

To start, one must understand the very limits of being a minor league franchise. Both historically and in contemporary analysis, these teams are almost habitually relegated to obscurity. More often than not, they are patted on the head as perfunctory stepping stones in the bigger picture of the game – places where emerging young stars graduate to the majors all too quickly, and washed up veterans languish for far too long. They're portrayed as teams with comically terrible names and mascots, playing in rundown stadiums to small, disinterested crowds.

Cultural depictions of minor league baseball mostly add to this image, for while major league stories are often recounted in serious efforts such as *61** and *Moneyball*, the minors are often relegated to serving as comical backdrops in the likes of *Bull Durham* and *Brockmire*. A 2014 issue of Mad Magazine carries on this perception with an admittedly hilarious fake minor league baseball flyer that "tells it like it is."

The ad, for the fictional Umber Falls Dirt Lobsters, boasts of new star players such as Biff Brocade (1974 A-League Rookie of the Year!) and promotions like "Half-Price Ice Water Day" and "Better Luck Next Year Foam Finger Night." And if you come out to see whatever longtime rival happens to be in their newly realigned division, you can meet their mascot Bisque, whose costume is now lice free!

Beyond the habitual ridicule minor league clubs often receive, they face unique challenges in maintaining consistent levels of respectable play and fan interest. Given that they serve as talent conduits for Major League Baseball, they only get to enjoy the services of their best players for abbreviated and unpredictable stretches of time. Thus, how can they not only hope to field consistently winning teams to keep people coming to the ballpark, but also have a memorable team identity that fans can grow attached to?

Additionally, if there are MLB franchises in the region, how can an A-ball squad sustain high attendance when locals could save their money and make the effort to see professional baseball at the "highest" level? Even the most successful affiliations with major league clubs don't last forever, as they're tied to contracts whose expirations can lead to frequent changes in MLB and A-league pairings. After all, while Sacramentans badly missed their beloved Solons for years, they still had MLB's Oakland Athletics and San Francisco Giants to see and root for less than two hours away.

Arguably, no franchise has exceeded these limitations and commanded respect like the Sacramento River Cats. A minor league franchise in name only, their history, while young, is unmatched by other AAA clubs in terms of producing major league stars and winning seasons of their own. For stars, there are enough examples to fill out a book of its own. As the AAA affiliate of MLB's Oakland Athletics, they provided the nucleus of talent for Billy Beane's "Moneyball" squads in the early 2000s, immortalized by Michael Lewis's book and the Oscar-nominated 2011 movie starring Brad Pitt as Beane.

This included vaunted starting pitchers Barry Zito and Mark Mulder, as well as position players like Miguel Tejada, Eric Byrnes, Ramon Hernandez, and Mark Ellis. When the A's returned to making the playoffs on a limited budget in 2012, 2013 and 2014, they did so on the strength of another crop of River Cats regulars that included Sonny Gray, Josh Donaldson and Eric Sogard.

It isn't just Oakland who has benefited from Sacramento's talent. The Boston Red Sox and Philadelphia Phillies won long-sought World Series titles thanks in part to the heroics of Mark Bellhorn and Joe Blanton respectively, with many other championship teams boasting former River Cats on their roster. Slugger Carlos Gonzalez has bolstered the Colorado Rockies' explosive offense for years with a bat that's won Silver Slugger and batting titles.

Ryan Ludwick's reliable offense helped everyone from the Texas Rangers to the 2012 Cincinnati Reds' 97-win postseason team, while the Washington Nationals' acclaimed starting rotation from 2012-2018 excelled thanks in no small part to Gio Gonzalez. Even before Sacramento became the AAA affiliate of the San Francisco Giants, River Cats alumni Santiago Casilla and Barry Zito helped the Boys from the Bay win a bundle of championships in 2010, 2012 and 2014.

However, being a training ground for an array of big-league stars like these doesn't overshadow what the team by the Sacramento River has accomplished on its own. In 20 seasons of play, they've won 12 division titles, five Pacific Coast League titles, seven Pacific Conference titles, and three AAA championships in 2007, 2008 and 2019. In 2012, the franchise was ranked by Forbes Magazine as the most valuable team in all of minor league baseball at $32 million.

Despite sharing a city with the popular NBA Kings franchise, they've never suffered from fan disinterest, leading all of Minor League Baseball in attendance year after year. According to Dan Vistica, the team's former executive vice president, the "mentality when we built, opened, and initially operated [the team] was while it was a minor league baseball team, he [owner Art Savage] wanted it to be a major league experience."

Indeed, the River Cats came to the River City with prestigious expectations in the minds of Sacramentans. After the second iteration of the Solons left town following the conclusion of the 1976 season, people in the city and the greater Central Valley region fought relentlessly for the next two decades to bring baseball back to the capital. When hopes of a major league franchise were supplanted by more realistic pushes for a minor league team, the expectation for a top-tier organization was still prevalent. After all, even before the arrival of MLB clubs in the '50s and '60s, California baseball thrived thanks to the Pacific Coast League, of which Sacramento was consistently an integral participant.

The dream came to fruition in the late '90s thanks chiefly to the actions of Art Savage, a veteran businessman from Los Angeles who spent most of the decade as president and CEO of the National Hockey League's San Jose Sharks. In a prescient moment as Savage readied for the Sharks' inaugural season, Dan Vistica (a friend of Savage's since the early '70s) declined an invitation to work in San Jose before adding: "But I'm gonna tell ya Art, I'm gonna look forward to the day when you purchase a professional baseball team, triple A presumably, and move it to Sacramento." Savage merely replied, "Oh Dan, you don't know what you're talking about."

Years later in October 1998, almost to the day of Vistica's promise, Savage called his old friend from Vancouver, Canada and announced, "Dan, I just purchased the Vancouver Canadians from a group of Japanese investors, and if everything goes well we will move that franchise to Sacramento in the next couple of years to bring baseball back after a 25-year absence." It was official: the city would have a new team just in time for the new millennium.

Savage's acquisition of the Canadians represented not only the culmination of two decades of trying to return baseball to Sacramento; it was also the ideal convergence of business figures and circumstances to allow the best possible team and stadium to be realized. To be sure, it wasn't even the first attempt to secure a team in the 1990s. In 1994, Fred Anderson attempted to secure a concrete bunker by Arco Arena for a single-A stadium, but the deal for a lesser team fell through. Gregg Lukenbill, who brought the

Kings to Sacramento and built their original arenas, attempted to secure the same site with likewise results.

But in 1997, Savage's last year as CEO of the Sharks, businessmen Bob Hemond and Warren Smith proposed bringing AAA baseball to West Sacramento. Savage soon arrived from San Jose and proved to be just the experienced figure necessary to guide them through some particularly trying hurdles. In one instance, a contentious all-day meeting with West Sacramento officials stretched to just before midnight. The two sides bickered back and forth over various issues before ending at an impasse. Hemond and Smith were frustrated and exhausted, both unable to sleep the rest of the night.

When they arrived at the office the next day in down spirits, Savage showed up spry and energetic. A stark contrast to the exhausted duo, the two incredulously asked Savage, "What's the deal, Art? We were up all night worrying. What are we going to do? How could you sleep?" The former Sharks owner curtly replied, "I slept like a baby. I took NyQuil."

Savage's cool attitude would ultimately be vindicated. By 1999 the group had financing, marketing, widespread support, and money for a new stadium situated along the Sacramento River right by the city's landmark Tower Bridge. Before throwing a pitch in California, the franchise came with a winning spirit already, winning the Triple-A World Series in 1999 while still in Vancouver.

Even in a city hungering for the return of local baseball, there were still obstacles to clear to guarantee the newly acquired franchise would take the field in 2000 as Savage envisioned. First was the task of building Raley Field on time, a process initially stymied by various delays. "There seemed to be an innumerable number of forces that were working against us," recalled Vistica. "There were lawsuits that were filed in terms of environmental matters, there were lawsuits filed on various other matters that really created significant delays in getting the financing in place, which created the delay in starting the project, and forced us basically to get this thing built in record-breaking time."

High interest rates in 1999 and 2000 further encumbered the financing process, while other delays came from lawsuits by those who still demanded the city receive a major league team. With bond financing officially secured in late August 1999, along with the full support of the city, an official naming sponsor courtesy of Raley's Supermarkets, and construction assigned to the local J.R. Roberts Construction, they finally broke ground around Labor Day. But a daunting task lay ahead, as a construction process that would normally take 18 months had to be completed in less than half that time in order to be ready for opening day in 2000.

Aside from the hurried construction process for Raley Field, the last task to coronate the team was to select its name. Rather than resurrect the Solons, team officials felt they should have a new name to honor their scenic location by the Sacramento River. After months of deliberation, it was thus decided that "Sacramento River" would be the first part of the name. The last part, in a sincere gesture to the locals who had desired baseball's return for over two decades, was determined in a contest for and by the fans.

Hundreds submitted their ideas, with the most popular choice being the Sacramento River Cats. Many ridiculed the moniker, but money would ultimately do the loudest talking, as the River Cats would go on to lead the minors in merchandise sales. It certainly beat suggestions like the River City Fighting Salmon, or the Sacramento Bureaucrats. Savage no doubt understood the value of a name early when the San Jose Sharks set records with a combination of a stellar logo and good play.

As miraculous as the ballpark's breakneck construction was, it still couldn't circumvent the reality that baseball begins in April. This didn't make its completion any less jaw-dropping, as an 18-month project ended up being finished in eight-and-a-half months. As Dan Vistica recalls, "From the time we broke ground until we were ready to open the facility, it really was almost a 24-hour, seven day a week process. We had something going on the site literally at all times."

In spite of this stressful task, the construction crews and subcontractors carried out the building with a blissful, "whistle-while-you-work" disposition. "When we would visit the site," recalled Warren Smith, one of the pivotal backers of the team's move to Sacramento, "the workers would tell us what a great place this would be." Impromptu decisions during the building process, such as building the clubhouses for the teams above ground rather than below, helped shave several months off the process as well. All the same, by April of 2000, long spells of rain further pushed back the deadline and the remaining odds and ends needed to ensure a stadium opening worthy of such an anticipated arrival.

Consequently, the home opener of the inaugural 2000 season for the River Cats, as well as the grand return of pro baseball to the city of Sacramento, had to be delayed until May. This forced the team to start the season with a historic 37-game road trip. By contrast, most normal road trips only last a week or so. The River Cats' extended road trip was surpassed in PCL history only by the Solons' 88-game sojourn in 1948. That, of course, was due to Edmonds Field burning to the ground, while the River Cats could at least look forward to an untouched gem of a new stadium.

By all accounts, the River Cats' long road trip is one no other team would ever want to endure. Despite emerging from the trip with a winning 22-15 record to start the season, each leg seemed to feature a new burden to add to the exhaustion of life on the road. A 36-hour flu bug picked up in Albuquerque, New Mexico hit six players as well as manager Bob Geren. A bus ride out of Fresno was delayed when the driver (who some coaches thought looked and sounded a lot like Cheech Marin) claimed his bus was stolen, only to suddenly remember he had taken it into the shop for repairs. Even when the team's schedule took them to Oakland for four "home" games in their MLB partner's stadium, their flight was delayed, and their Holiday Inn rooms weren't ready upon their arrival.

An aerial view of Raley Field. Photo courtesy of Alan O'Connor.

When the real home opener finally arrived on May 15, however, the anticipation wasn't the least bit dissipated. For the team, it was as much a relief as it was a festive occasion. Their 2:22 PM arrival at Sacramento International Airport officially concluded a traveling grind that spanned 40 days, 41 nights, and 37 games. For the fans of Sacramento, a wait of two-and-a-half decades was about to come to an end.

"The build-up in the community, the anticipation, the excitement, the 'we can't wait' feeling was absolutely amazing," recalled Dan Vistica. "Media coverage, electronic and print, was incredible." Not even a sudden inch and a half of rare late spring rain from 4:30 to 6:00 could spoil the festivities, but only push them back a hair. Thanks to the field's drainage system, pregame ceremonies and dignitary intros still took place, and the first pitch was only delayed from its original 7:05 time to 7:40.

The River Cats lost the game 2-1 to the Edmonton Trappers, but fans were hooked. That summer, featuring many home stands to compensate for the opening road trip, witnessed seemingly endless sellouts. Even on July 15, with nearby competition such as the A's-Giants Bay Bridge series, the WNBA's Monarchs at Arco Arena, and Summer Olympic trials at Cal State University, Raley Field was teeming at full capacity for the tenth straight game.

Just as the inaugural season had started too late in Sacramento, it would likewise end too soon. A late-season swoon was followed by a quick exit from the playoffs on the road in Salt Lake City, depriving fans of a home field goodbye.

But a 90-54 regular season record, with a once in a lifetime summer that witnessed 67 home games in just 109 days, marked an unqualified success. Additionally, the Cats won consistently even as many key players like Barry Zito and Eric Byrnes were shuffled back and forth to Oakland, who also made the MLB playoffs in 2000. To say the least, the promise of an outstanding baseball franchise had been resoundingly established.

Since then, that promise has been fulfilled, as the River Cats have been quick and unwavering in attaining new heights of on-field success. Only three years later in 2003, they claimed their first PCL championship, a moment no one in the organization took for granted. Recalls Vistica: "We knew that so many franchises had not won a championship. So to win that first one and see Art and the team and Gary Arthur, our general manager at the time, out on the field in the celebration was pretty special. Then to go back-to-back and win again in 2004, and that year we actually clinched and won the pennant and PCL championship in Iowa...I had the opportunity to be in Iowa for that, and while it wasn't at home it was still very, very special."

Barry Zito prepares to deliver a pitch during the River Cats' inaugural 2000 season, in which he was called up to the Oakland Athletics. Photo courtesy of the Sacramento River Cats.

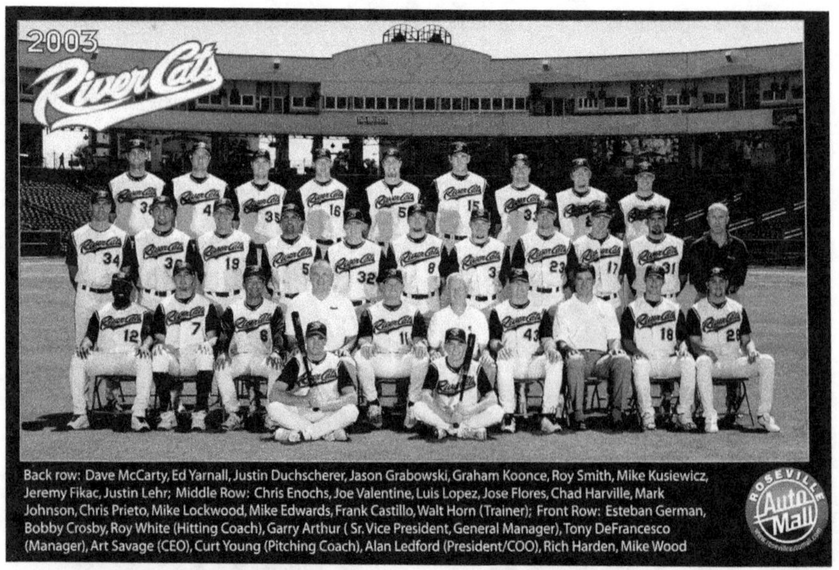

Back row: Dave McCarty, Ed Yarnall, Justin Duchscherer, Jason Grabowski, Graham Koonce, Roy Smith, Mike Kusiewicz, Jeremy Fikac, Justin Lehr; Middle Row: Chris Enochs, Joe Valentine, Luis Lopez, Jose Flores, Chad Harville, Mark Johnson, Chris Prieto, Mike Lockwood, Mike Edwards, Frank Castillo, Walt Horn (Trainer); Front Row: Esteban German, Bobby Crosby, Roy White (Hitting Coach), Garry Arthur (Sr. Vice President, General Manager), Tony DeFrancesco (Manager), Art Savage (CEO), Curt Young (Pitching Coach), Alan Ledford (President/COO), Rich Harden, Mike Wood

The 2003 River Cats, winners of the first PCL crown by any Sacramento team since the 1942 Solons. Photo courtesy of Alan O'Connor.

Additionally, the '03 title was the first PCL pennant by a Sacramento team since the hallowed 1942 Solons. A brief reprieve in 2005 and 2006 was quickly followed by the team's crowning years of 2007 and 2008, where they won not only the PCL championship both years but also the reinstated AAA baseball title.

The 2007 championship campaign in particular embodied everything that distinguishes the River Cats. There were shades of the 1942 Solons when they fell behind 2-0 in the first round of the playoffs against Salt Lake City. But the River Cats rallied to win the next three to take the series. Game four was decided by a walk-off home run by Danny Putnam that echoed Gene Lillard's blast in 1942. They proceeded to knock off the New Orleans Zephyrs in three games to claim their third PCL crown, and finished things by defeating the Richmond Braves for their first ever AAA championship.

The River Cats celebrate the 2007 PCL title at Raley Field. Owner Art Savage can be seen in the bottom right team photo. (Bottom row, kneeling third from left.) Photo courtesy of the Sacramento Public Library and Sacramento River Cats.

Celebration of the River Cats' 2007 title run even echoed in the halls of Congress in Washington, D.C. In a speech before the House of Representatives on October 16, Congresswoman Doris Matsui recognized the team's accomplishment in great detail, praising their resilience despite so many players being called up to Oakland (180 roster changes in total). She effusively praised the leadership of Art Savage and manager Tony DeFrancesco, as well as the enormous attendance that supported the team all season long. "I ask all my colleagues to join me in celebrating the River Cats 2007 championship season," she concluded.

For Vistica, 2007 was a signature year for the franchise not only for bringing home their first AAA championship, but for a special moment that occurred just before in September. As Oakland expanded its roster from 25 players to 40, left-handed reliever Jerry Blevins (known as "Baby Koufax" for his resemblance to Dodgers legend Sandy Koufax) was promoted to the majors for the first time.

As Vistica recounts: "We had a little gathering in what we call our Solon Club, and we invited the players primarily because [manager] Tony DeFrancesco wanted to make a very special announcement at the end of that game. And that was that: Jerry Blevins had been called up to Oakland, and to see a grown man and his reaction to that moment, his first call-up to the major leagues, that was pretty special. And those types of moments are the ones that are kind of 'behind the scenes,' that people don't see or hear about, but are really, really special."

This story, while capturing the authentic joy of succeeding in baseball, also perfectly encapsulates the most remarkable part of Sacramento's success. From 2000 to 2014, they almost always contended while constantly meeting the needs of the Oakland Athletics, a team that relies on minor league talent due to its perennially low budgets and revenues. To such an extent that as Dan Vistica noted in an interview: "We've had years where we've had over 200 transactions of players in and out of our roster. So when a player's called up to Oakland, that's one transaction, when they come back down that's another one. When we call up a player from Midland, which is the A's' AA affiliate, that's a transaction. That's really a significant amount of movement. But what it's done is it's created an opportunity really for some of the younger players to showcase their talent here at the triple A level and allow them to move on to Oakland, and in many cases other major league teams."

While the 2014 season witnessed more synchronicity between the A's and River Cats winning, Sacramento had to be ready for a tremendous change. After their contract with Oakland expired at season's end, the team made the highly popular decision to switch to the San Francisco Giants as their next affiliate. The Giants, despite barely making the playoffs as a second wild card team, had beaten the odds to win yet another World Series, their third in five years. In addition to Sacramento's steady stream of upcoming talent, fans at Raley Field have since had the privilege of seeing Giants stars like Madison Bumgarner and Hunter Pence don the River Cats uniform while rehabbing from injuries.

Regardless of the success and popularity of the MLB franchise they're tethered to, the Sacramento River Cats excel enough on their own to command respect as a top-tier professional ball club. While the Senators and Solons of the previous century hosted many talented players and had their share of winning teams, they often languished in the middle or the cellar of the standings. The River Cats, meanwhile, have been a winning or first place team on an almost annual basis. Their success has done more than satiate the appetites of fans who waited two and a half decades for professional baseball to return to the city.

Ultimately, they mark the culmination of a rich lineage of baseball that began in the 1860s with the California State Fair and a visit from the Cincinnati Red Stockings, blossomed with the Altas and Gilt Edge, went through decades of peaks and valleys with the Senators and Solons, and then seemingly died save for the brief reprise of the '70s Solons. Given their popularity and success in almost two full decades of operation, including another AAA championship in 2019 and new stadium name sponsorship from Sutter Health starting in 2020, it's safe to surmise they're here to stay.

TWELVE

HOME FIELD ADVANTAGE – 50 BASEBALL GREATS WHO HERALD FROM AND PLAYED IN SACRAMENTO

A baseball player's hometown can add a dimension to their story that deepens the resonance of their on-field accomplishments. In some instances, a player's humble origins provide a perfect juxtaposition to his majestic reputation in the major leagues. Take Mickey Mantle, the blonde, all-American boy from a small town who became the game's premiere superstar with its most hallowed franchise, the New York Yankees. But before launching home runs to the thrill of millions in America's biggest city, he honed his swing with a tin shed for a backstop in Commerce, Oklahoma, a town whose population doesn't exceed 3,000.

Others returned to their hometown for their greatest achievement, perhaps the best such story being that of pitcher Jack Morris. Despite being the winningest starter of the 1980s for the Detroit Tigers, Morris was repeatedly denied the chance to pursue free agency by owner collusion. Finally, after 13 years in the majors with just one team, the St. Paul, MN native signed with the Minnesota Twins in February of 1991. Morris teared up at the press conference, overwhelmed by the chance to play for the team he grew up watching. Months later, in front of over 50,000 roaring hometown fans, he pitched all ten innings of game seven in a dramatic World Series to bring home Minnesota's second World Series championship.

Given Sacramento's rich history of professional baseball, as well as its prominence at each phase of the sport's growth in California, it's unsurprisingly been home to dozens of renowned players, managers and coaches. Some were born in the city and moved on to major league success. Others heralded from elsewhere, but had a stint with the Senators, Solons or River Cats to sharpen their skills, or attended a local school. And of course, there are the "consummate" figures who were born in Sacramento and grew up and played baseball there. A few others came to Sacramento with their major league days behind them, only to find new success in a Solons uniform.

This chapter, by no means exhaustive, details 50 of the greatest baseball figures with a Sacramento connection. World Series heroes, All-Stars, no-hit and perfect game pitchers, Hall of Famers, respected managers and coaches, comeback players, beloved fan favorites: every kind of baseball hero has a path that started in, or eventually weaved through, Sacramento.

Author's Note: Individuals from nearby towns like Davis, Folsom and Woodland are included in this list. The following 50 are listed in alphabetical order by last name.

1.　DUSTY BAKER

Born on June 15, 1949, in Riverside, CA, Johnnie B. "Dusty" Baker excelled as a multi-sport athlete at Del Campo High School in Fair Oaks. He earned a selection by the Atlanta Braves in the 1967 MLB Amateur Draft, right out of high school. Suiting up as an outfielder for the Braves from 1968-1975, he distinguished himself as a powerful hitter, batting .321 in 1972 and hitting 20 or more homers the next two seasons. However, Baker became frustrated by Atlanta's lack of postseason contention, as well as their decision to trade his mentor, Hank Aaron, to Milwaukee. He asked to be traded to a West Coast team and was thus dealt to the Los Angeles Dodgers in November 1975.

It was the perfect destination for Baker, a Dodger fan since his youth who was coached by team legend Spider Jorgensen while playing for the Fair Oaks American Legion team. From 1976 to 1983, he earned two All-Star selections (1981, 1982), one Gold Glove (1981), two Silver Slugger Awards (1980, 1981), 1977 National League Championship Series Most Valuable Player, and was a member of the 1981 World Series championship team. His 30 home runs in 1977 contributed to a unique feat, making that year's Dodgers team the first in baseball history to have four players to hit at least 30 home runs (the other three being Ron Cey, Steve Garvey and Reggie Smith).

A few years after his playing days ended in 1986, Baker began a successful managing career with the San Francisco Giants in 1993, leading them to the World Series in 2002, the Chicago Cubs to the National League Championship Series in 2003, the Cincinnati Reds to three playoff appearances (2010, 2012, 2013) after a 15-year postseason drought, and the Washington Nationals to the playoffs in 2016 and 2017 after their disastrous 2015 season.

His career as a skipper boasts three National League Manager of the

FUN FACTS

While accomplished as a player and manager, Baker also has the distinction of being one of the greatest footnotes in baseball history. On April 8, 1974, in an Atlanta Braves home game against the Dodgers, he was standing on deck when Hank Aaron hit his 715th career home run, surpassing Babe Ruth to become the all-time MLB home run leader.

Recalled Baker, "I'm on my way up to the plate once they resumed play, and I heard a bunch of clanking ... and I looked around, everybody was leaving. They were going home and saw what they came to see. So then I hit a double." Baker's recollection is just a bit off, however: he actually drew a walk after Aaron's milestone shot. But he did double in Aaron beforehand in the second inning.

It wasn't the only fascinating story of Baker's long career. In 1977, when he, Cey, Smith, and Garvey all hit 30 home runs, they took a photo with the number 30 on the Dodger Stadium scoreboard behind them. The only problem: Baker had yet to hit his 30th when it was taken. But on the last day of the regular season, facing Houston Astros ace J.R. Richard, he clubbed his record-setting blast in the sixth inning.

Then, upon touching home plate, he was greeted by teammate Glenn Burke, who held his hand in the air. Baker responded with what some believe is the first "high five." Whether or not Baker and Burke did in fact "invent" the now universal gesture, the legend has stuck, even being referenced in an episode of the popular cartoon *American Dad*.

Year awards (1993, 1997, 2000), all while managing the Giants. Baker was inducted into the Sacramento Sports Hall of Fame in 2013, and currently works as a special advisor for San Francisco. He is also co-owner of Baker Family Wines, which is slated to open a tasting room soon across from Bike Dog Brewing in West Sacramento.

Baker observes batting practice at Pacific Bell Park in San Francisco before game three of the 2002 World Series. Photo by Julie Jacobson, courtesy of the Associated Press.

2. GENE BEARDEN

Hailing from Lexa, Arkansas, Henry Eugene Bearden lived an idyllic baseball childhood. He learned to play the game in sandlots in Tennessee, while idolizing Yankees legend Lou Gehrig. Pitching for various minor league organizations, Bearden joined the Navy during World War II before being able to graduate to the major leagues. But on July 6, 1943, those big-league dreams were threatened when his ship, the *USS Helena*, was attacked by Japanese torpedoes near the Solomon Islands. As the ship sank and claimed 168 lives, Bearden managed to survive, albeit with brutal injuries. When he was found drifting across the water in a life raft, his head had been smashed open, and one of his knees reduced to a chunk of wounded flesh.

He spent the next two years recuperating in hospitals, having a silver plate inserted into his skull and a metal hinge placed in his damaged knee. In spite of constant pain that seemed to negate a return to baseball, Bearden nonetheless went straight back to the diamond after his discharge in 1945. He proved he was more than able right away with 15 wins in 1945 for the Yankees' farm team in Binghamton, NY. The next season, Bearden further excelled with the Oakland Oaks of the Pacific Coast League, racking up another 15 wins under the guidance of future Hall of Fame manager Casey Stengel. Thanks to Stengel's help, he was able to develop his signature pitch, the knuckleball.

In December of 1946, Bearden was shipped to the Cleveland Indians in a massive trade, making his major league debut the next season on May 10, 1947. He was promptly shelled in his lone appearance, giving him an earned run average of 81.00 and a ticket back to Oakland to work on his mechanics for the rest of the season. While Bearden managed to pitch excellently during that stretch, he seemed a far cry from belonging in the same company as fellow Cleveland pitchers Bob Feller, Bob Lemon and Steve Gromek. Even after earning a spot on the roster for the 1948 season in spring training, he didn't make a start until May 8.

Easily defeating the Washington Senators 6-1, Bearden's reputation soared thereafter as he continued to pile up wins throughout the season. All the while, the Indians locked horns with the Boston Red Sox in a tight pennant race, and by September 16, both were dead even at 87 wins.

Player-manager Lou Boudreau, even with more established aces like Feller, Lemon and Satchel Paige at his disposal, chose Bearden as Cleveland's go-to ace down the last stretch of the season. In an incredible run, the pitcher who seemed unlikely to play after war injuries just five years prior proceeded to start five of the remaining 15 games of the regular season, winning every single one.

Especially in today's era of pitching, where a single start on three days' rest is considered a challenge, Bearden's ability to win five games with minimal rest is even more awe-inspiring. The last of these five wins came on October 2, an 8-0 shutout of the Detroit Tigers that clinched a tie with the Red Sox for the American League pennant. Thus, the season came down to a one-game playoff on Monday, October 4, to determine who would advance to the World Series. Once again, Boudreau eagerly tapped Bearden on short rest, a decision that received widespread derision in the baseball press. Aside from pitching on incredibly short notice yet again, Bearden would have to pitch in Fenway Park in Boston, a stadium where left-handed pitchers generally struggled.

Despite pre-game jitters, he showed no sign of fatigue, cutting the Red Sox offense to shreds with this signature knuckleball in a pennant-winning 8-3 victory. His teammates joyously carried him of the field in celebration, a stirring antithesis to the moment he washed ashore in a life raft with gaping wounds. It was on to the World Series against the Boston Braves, where Bearden had yet more pitching mastery to spin. Starting in game three with the series tied a game apiece, he shut out the Braves 2-0, all while aiding his cause at the plate with a double and a single.

It all came down to one more heroic stand in game six, with Cleveland leading three-games-to-two and needing just one more win for their first championship since 1920. Bob Lemon, who pitched magnificently and was staked to a 4-1 lead, loaded the bases in the bottom of the eighth inning. Bearden, with only three days' rest, was tapped by Boudreau for one more dramatic effort. While the Braves managed to score two runs, Bearden escaped the jam and recorded the last three outs in the 9th inning, securing the World Series for Cleveland.

While Bearden wasn't able to parlay his storybook 1948 season into a standout career, he did manage a brief spell of success in a Solons uniform before hanging up the cleats for good. Taking to the pitcher's mound for the 1956 team, he enjoyed a 15-14 record and a 3.48 ERA as the Solons managed to finish .500 in a decade that often saw them in the cellar. In spite of the initial severity of his war injuries, Bearden lived a fulfilling life all the way to age 83 before he passed away on March 18, 2004, in Alexander City, Alabama.

3. MARK BELLHORN

Mark Christian Bellhorn was born in 1974 in Boston, Massachusetts, but grew up primarily in Orlando, Florida. After graduating from Oviedo High School, Bellhorn played baseball for the Auburn Tigers from 1993 to 1996, playing in the 1994 College World Series during that stretch. He debuted in the majors with the Oakland Athletics in 1997, but generally saw limited playing time through the 2001 season. During his time with the Athletics organization, Bellhorn had significant stretches in a River Cats uniform, being most visible at Raley Field during their inaugural 2000 season. Taking the field in 117 games, he notched a .266 batting average, 11 triples, 24 home runs, and 73 RBIs.

In only 46 games as a River Cat in 2001, Bellhorn hit .269 with 12 homers and 36 RBIs. After playing with the Chicago Cubs and Colorado Rockies in 2002-2003, Bellhorn's finest hour came in 2004 with his hometown Boston Red Sox. In the regular season, he accomplished career high marks in batting average (.264) and RBIs (82), although he also led the league in strikeouts (177).

His postseason numbers got off to a glacial start, but his bat would come alive just in time to assist the greatest comeback in baseball history. Facing the arch rival New York Yankees in the American League Championship Series, Boston once again seemed headed for another playoff heartbreak after the Yankees took a three-games-to-none lead. Two white-knuckle walk-off wins in games four and five in Boston sent the series back to New York, where Bellhorn rose to the occasion.

In the fourth inning of game six, Bellhorn stepped to the plate with Jason Varitek and Orlando Cabrera on base. He promptly launched a Jon Lieber pitch into the left field stands, although it was originally ruled as in play since it appeared to strike a fan. When the umpiring crew correctly overruled it as a home run, it gave injured starter Curt Schilling all of the offense he would need in a 4-2 win. In the deciding game seven, Bellhorn added to Boston's cathartic 10-3 pounding of their hated rivals, blasting a booming homer off the right field foul pole in the eighth inning.

Even with the first 3-0 comeback in baseball history completed, Boston still had the challenge of facing the St. Louis Cardinals, baseball's winningest team in 2004, in the World Series. Game one in Boston was a seesaw affair, with both teams scoring back and forth. After St. Louis tied the game at nine in the top of eighth inning, Bellhorn stepped to the plate in the bottom half with Varitek on base and Julian Tavarez on the mound for the Cardinals.

After a ball and two strikes, Bellhorn proceeded to lace a towering hit down the right field line, bouncing off the famous "Pesky Pole" for a go-ahead home run. It ended up being the winning hit of the only competitive game of the series, as Boston dominated the next three to complete a sweep for their first championship since 1918. Bellhorn would spend until 2007 bouncing from team to team, taking the field for the Yankees, Padres and Reds before retiring.

4. JOE BLANTON

Joseph Matthew Blanton was born in 1980 in Nashville, Tennessee, and grew up primarily in Kentucky. After his education at Franklin-Simpson High School and University of Kentucky, Blanton was selected in the 2002 MLB Draft by the Oakland Athletics as part of their famous "Moneyball" class. He pitched extensively for the River Cats in 2004, winning 11 games and striking out 143 batters in 176.1 innings pitched as Sacramento won the Pacific Coast League title. Making his A's debut in September 2004, Blanton pitched respectably for the next three seasons, managing .500 or better records although his ERA generally stayed above 4.00.

However, Blanton stumbled in the first half of 2008 with a subpar record of 5-12 and a 4.96 ERA, thus being dealt to the Philadelphia Phillies on July 17. After donning red pinstripes, he helped contribute to the play-off-bound Phillies by going 4-0 in the second half of the season as the team clinched its second National League East Division championship in a row. In the National League Division Series against the Milwaukee Brewers, Blanton stamped Philadelphia's ticket to the next round of the playoffs with seven strikeouts and only one run allowed in six innings of work in game four. After dismissing the Los Angeles Dodgers in the National League Championship Series, the Phillies advanced to face the Tampa Bay Rays in the World Series, where Blanton would realize his greatest, and most unlikely, moment.

With Philadelphia leading the series two-games-to-one, Blanton gave a consummate effort as their game four pitcher. He allowed only two runs over six innings pitched, while aiding the offense's ten-run onslaught with a solo home run in the bottom of the fifth inning. This made him the first pitcher to hit a home run in the World Series since Ken Holtzman of the Oakland Athletics in 1974. The Phillies sealed the championship in the next game at home, their first World Series title in 28 years.

Also pitching in the 2009 World Series, as well as the 2010 and 2011 post-seasons for Philadelphia, Blanton has since taken the field for the Dodgers, Los Angeles Angels of Anaheim, and Kansas City Royals. Another notable highlight for the righty came on September 25, 2016, being the winning pitcher of the Dodgers' NL West Division clincher that also marked hallowed announcer Vin Scully's last game at Dodger Stadium as the team's announcer.

5. JEFF BLAUSER

Born in Los Gatos, California in 1965, Jeffrey Michael Blauser attended Placer High School in Auburn and Sacramento City College before being selected in the 1984 amateur draft by the Atlanta Braves. Despite some issues defensively, Blauser made a name for himself as a power-hitting right-handed shortstop for Atlanta teams that frequently appeared in the playoffs. A two-time All-Star (1993, 1997) and 1997 Silver Slugger Award recipient, Blauser was a member of four National League pennant-winning Braves teams (1991, 1992, 1995, 1996), with the 1995 squad winning the World Series. He closed out his career with two seasons for the Chicago Cubs, 1998-1999.

6. CHRIS BOSIO

Born in Carmichael in 1963, Christopher Louis Bosio attended Cordova High School and Sacramento City College before being drafted in the second round of the 1982 MLB Amateur Draft by the Milwaukee Brewers. He took to the pitcher's mound with Milwaukee (1986-1992) and the Seattle Mariners (1993-1996). His finest moment as a player occurred on April 22, 1993, when he became the second pitcher in Mariners history to throw a no-hitter, blanking the Boston Red Sox at the Seattle Kingdome.

His greatest accomplishment overall, however, would come later as pitching coach of the Chicago Cubs. After taking the position in 2012, the first year of general manager Theo Epstein's rebuild of the team, Bosio oversaw a pitching staff that turned the "Loveable Losers" into one of the best teams in the game in 2015. It all culminated the following year in 2016, when the Cubs' MLB-best pitching staff led the team to 103 wins and the franchise's first World Series title since 1908.

After Chicago secured their title in a white-knuckle 8-7, ten-inning win in game seven, Bosio received congratulations on social media from former colleagues and Sacramento locals for his part in ending the Cubs' staggering 108-year drought. He was inducted into the Sacramento Sports Hall of Fame in 2019.

7. LARRY BOWA

Born in Sacramento on December 6, 1945, Lawrence Robert Bowa had baseball in his blood from the very beginning. His father Paul played in the minors (including the Solons in 1944), while his mother Mary excelled at softball. He started learning the game in his childhood with Land Park Little League, with his father tutoring him every step of the way.

Boasting a small, skinny frame that always ensured he was the smallest player on the squad, he was quick to learn how to overcome adversity as much as he rehearsed baseball fundamentals. Bowa later attended C.K. McClatchy High School, where the school coach curtly told him he was too short to play baseball and cut him from the squad.

A young Bowa (colored red) while playing for Land Park Little League. Photo courtesy of the Sac City Express.

Undeterred, he continued to hone his craft in Summer League, eventually earning a roster spot with the Sacramento City College Panthers. His hard work paid off by winning league MVP, as well as the attention of Philadelphia Phillies scout Eddie Bockman. He would go on to play shortstop from 1970-1985 for the Phillies, Chicago Cubs and New York Mets.

Bowa garnered numerous accolades during his 15-year career, including five All-Star selections with the Phillies (1974, 1975, 1976, 1978, 1979), National League leader in fielding percentage six times, 2,191 career hits, and Gold Gloves in 1972 and 1978. Renowned as one of the game's top defensive wizards, he once held the record for most games played at shortstop in the National League.

Bowa takes a swing while practicing for the SJC Panthers in 1964. Photo courtesy of the Sac City Express.

Complementing his defensive acumen was a fiery temperament and passion on the field, making him an integral figure of the Phillies' greatest run of success to date in the late '70s. Starting in 1976, the team went from perennial cellar-dwellers to a championship contender, and it all came together in 1980. Bowa was a spark plug that year, batting .316 in the National League Championship Series against the Houston Astros, highlighted by a clutch hit against Nolan Ryan in the eighth inning of game five that ignited a rally. After Philadelphia won perhaps the greatest NLCS ever played, he hit .375 in the World Series against the Kansas City Royals as the "Fightin' Phils" won their first World Series in franchise history.

Bowa throws to first to complete a double play in game one of the 1980 NLCS against the Houston Astros, at Veterans Stadium in Philadelphia, PA. Photo courtesy of the Associated Press.

After retiring as a player, he later became the manager of the Phillies, winning 2001 National League Manager of the Year. Bowa has also coached many teams, serving as bench coach recently in Philadelphia before moving to the front office. He was inducted into the Philadelphia Baseball Wall of Fame in 1991 and the Sacramento Sports Hall of Fame in 2016.

8. DALLAS BRADEN

Born in 1983 in Phoenix, Arizona, Dallas Lee Braden played Little League and high school baseball in Stockton. Losing his mother to cancer during his senior year, he lived with his maternal grandmother, Peggy Lindsey, and moved on to college baseball. First notching two excellent seasons at American River College, he proceeded to pitch for Texas Tech University before being selected by the Oakland Athletics in the 2004 MLB Draft. After pitching several years in single and double-A ball, Braden moved up briefly to the River Cats in 2007 en route to his MLB debut in Oakland that season. He struggled in his first two seasons and spent additional time in Sacramento in 2008.

A photo of Braden from a 2008 River Cats yearbook. Photo courtesy of the Sacramento Public Library and the Sacramento River Cats.

His inconsistency as a starter even became a target in a highly publicized feud with Yankees star Alex Rodriguez in 2010, after Rodriguez irked Braden by walking across the pitcher's mound on his way back to first base after a foul ball. When Braden blasted him for breaking the "unwritten rule" of only the pitcher walking across the mound, Rodriguez retorted, "That was a little surprising. I'd never quite heard that, especially from a guy that has a handful of wins in his career."

However, Braden would have the final word mere days later when he joined one of the most prestigious groups of baseball achievement on May 9, 2010. Facing the Tampa Bay Rays in Oakland, Braden threw the 19th perfect game in MLB history, an accomplishment made all the more poignant as it occurred on Mother's Day. While his mother wasn't alive to share the moment, his grandmother was on hand to celebrate, embracing her grandson on the field after his pitching masterpiece. As of this writing, Braden's perfect game is one of only 23 pitched in Major League Baseball history. After his playing career ended, Braden has worked as an analyst, most recently for A's broadcasts.

9. DOLPH CAMILLI

Adolph Louis "Dolph" Camilli was born on April 23, 1907, in San Francisco. His professional baseball career began 19 years later with his hometown Seals of the Pacific Coast League. His eight-year minor league career included a spell with the Sacramento Senators from 1929 to 1933, making his major league debut with the Chicago Cubs in September of 1933 as a first baseman. After being traded to the Philadelphia Phillies in June of 1934, he began to flourish offensively, blasting 25 or more home runs a year from 1935 to 1937, in addition to a career-high .339 batting average and the highest on-base percentage in the National League in 1937. However, Camilli's slugging ways came with a hefty strikeout rate, setting a league record in 1935 with 113.

Another trade in 1938 sent him from Philadelphia to the struggling Brooklyn Dodgers, who general manager Larry MacPhail was seeking to transform from cellar dwellers into a World Series contender. Camilli played an integral role in that turnaround, hitting more than 20 home runs every year from 1938 through 1942 and 100 or more RBIs every year except 1940. It all culminated in an incredible 1941 season, in which Camilli walloped a league-leading 34 home runs and 120 RBIs, earning his second All-Star selection and National League Most Valuable Player. Most importantly, his muscular bat helped power the Dodgers to their first National League pennant since 1920.

Camilli was traded yet again to the New York Giants in 1943, but refused to play for Brooklyn's arch rivals, opting instead to return to the Pacific Coast League as manager of the Oakland Oaks. After retiring from the majors following a stint with the Boston Red Sox in 1945, Camilli headed to the Pacific Coast League once more to work as a manager. In addition to the Oaks, he served as a coach for the Sacramento Solons in 1947 and 1955.

With major league career totals of 239 home runs, 950 RBIs and a career .277 batting average, Camilli later earned recognition for his accomplishments. He was inducted into the Dodgers Hall of Fame in 1984, as well as the Sacramento Athletic Hall of Fame. He passed away at age 90 on October 22, 1997, in San Mateo, CA.

10. SANTIAGO CASILLA

A native of San Cristobal in the Dominican Republic, Santiago Casilla has spent his entire professional career in Northern California, working as a relief pitcher for the Oakland Athletics and San Francisco Giants. Signed as an amateur free agent by Oakland in 2000, he spent significant stints with the River Cats every year of his tenure in the A's organization from 2004 to 2009. After his sometimes abbreviated and mostly inconsistent years in Oakland, he signed as a free agent with the San Francisco Giants for the 2010 season, and quickly flourished as one of the pillars of their renowned bullpen.

Going 7-2 with a 1.95 ERA in his first year as a Giant, Casilla became a stalwart reliever capable of filling any role. Often working as a setup man, he could serve as closer when needed, notching a career-high 25 saves in 2012. This versatility made him a key to the 2010, 2012 and 2014 Giants World Series championship teams, amassing a sparkling 0.95 ERA, 20 strikeouts and four saves through nine dramatic postseason series. Casilla enjoyed the prestige of being the winning pitcher of game four of the 2012 World Series, a 10-inning battle that sealed San Francisco's sweep of the Detroit Tigers. Following a disappointing 2016, a year when the entire Giants bullpen struggled mightily, Casilla re-signed with Oakland in the offseason.

11. JOSH DONALDSON

Hailing from Pensacola, Florida, Joshua Adam Donaldson initially honed his baseball skills in the Deep South with the Auburn Tigers. The Chicago Cubs drafted him in 2007 before trading him to the Oakland Athletics next year in a blockbuster deal to get pitching ace Rich Harden. Spending 2009 with the AA Midland RockHounds, Donaldson quickly announced himself as an exciting forthcoming star with the River Cats in 2010 and 2011. In 2010, despite a mere .238 average, he blasted 18 home runs and 67 RBIs. He significantly improved his line in 2011 to .261 with 17 homers and 70 RBIs, earning a call-up to play third base for the Athletics in 2012.

Donaldson on the base paths at Raley Field. Photo courtesy of the Sacramento River Cats.

Despite early struggles and another stint with the River Cats, Donaldson was recalled in August and solidified himself as their everyday third baseman after Brandon Inge's injury. He finished the year with nine home runs and 33 RBIs, boosting Oakland's improbable run to the American League West Division title. 2013 started with a bang for Donaldson, hitting his first walk-off home run on April 12 and his first career grand slam on June 7. He finished the year with a .301 batting average, 24 home runs and 93 RBIs, finishing fourth in American League Most Valuable Player voting and helping the Athletics win their division for the second year in a row.

In 2014, Donaldson earned his first All-Star selection, starting third base for the American League at the midsummer classic in Minneapolis, MN. While he would end that season with 29 home runs and 98 RBIs (even as his average sank to .255), the "Bringer of Rain" also flashed defensive prowess to match his powerful bat, winning his first ever Fielding Bible Award. This consummate talent led him to be ranked third in wins above replacement (WAR) in all of baseball in 2014, trailing league MVP's Clayton Kershaw and Mike Trout.

Despite his quick rise to elite status as a player, as well as immense popularity with the Oakland fanbase, Donaldson was traded to the Toronto Blue Jays that November as part of another ambitious "Moneyball" roster overhaul. He responded by blossoming even further, winning American League MVP in 2015 and leading the Blue Jays to the postseason for the first time since 1993. His bat would lead the Blue Jays to the ALCS a second year in a row in 2016, batting .538 in the ALDS against Texas and scoring the series-winning walk-off run in game three. Donaldson followed that by helping the Cleveland Indians to a third consecutive American League Central Division title in 2018, and the Atlanta Braves to their second straight National League East Division title in 2019.

12. JERMAINE DYE

Born in Oakland in 1974, Jermaine Trevell Dye grew up across Northern California, attending Will C. Wood High School in Vacaville and playing baseball at Cosumnes River College in Sacramento. Drafted by the Atlanta Braves in 1993, Dye opened his career with a bang on May 17, 1996, launching a home run in his first major league at-bat in Atlanta. He'd finish the season with an impressive 12 homers, 37 RBIs and a .281 batting average as the Braves reached the World Series for the second year in a row, with Dye participating in each playoff series.

After being traded to the Kansas City Royals the following year, he patrolled right field in Kauffman Stadium to great success and popularity.

In addition to earning his first All-Star selection and a Gold Glove in 2000, he became a beloved fan favorite in Kansas City, with fans chanting "Dye-no-mite!" whenever he stepped to the plate. A midseason trade in 2001 sent him to Oakland, where he further excelled with the revolutionary "Moneyball" Athletics and help them reach the postseason in 2001, 2002 and 2003. During this time, he played brief stints with the River Cats in '02 and '03.

After signing with the Chicago White Sox as a free agent, the powerful right-hander would achieve his greatest heroics in 2005. It was that season that the White Sox advanced to their first World Series since 1959, hoping to win their first championship since 1917. Dye rose to the occasion, batting .438 with a home run and 3 RBIs as the White Sox swept the Houston Astros for their first title in 88 years. He sealed the championship with an RBI single off Houston closer (and Sacramento native) Brad Lidge in the eighth inning of game four, earning World Series Most Valuable Player as a result.

Dye's best regular season came the following year in 2006, with totals of 44 home runs, 120 RBIs, a .315 batting average, and a .622 slugging average to earn his second All-Star selection and a Silver Slugger Award. After his 2007 season was marred by a slow first half, he roared back to help the White Sox win the American League Central Division in 2008, slashing 34 home runs alongside a .292 batting average. Throughout his career, Dye was renowned for right-handed power hitting at the plate and a cannon arm in the outfield, finishing with 325 career home runs upon retirement in 2011.

13. BRUCE EDWARDS

Charles Bruce Edwards was born in Quincy, Illinois on July 15, 1923. By his teen years, his family moved out west to Sacramento, where he would attend Sacramento High School. At only age 17, Edwards signed a deal with the Brooklyn Dodgers in 1941 after a successful tryout in San Mateo, CA. Changing from outfielder to catcher throughout his time in the minor leagues, his path to the majors was briefly interrupted by military service in World War II. After three years in a tank destroyer unit in Holland, France and Germany, Edwards resumed his career with the AA-class Mobile Bears.

The Dodgers, desperately searching for reliable help at catcher, called him up for his first major league game on June 23, 1946. Edwards proceeded to lace an RBI double in his first at-bat, kicking off a year in which he displayed offensive prowess as well as incredible durability behind home plate. He would end up catching 91 games in 1946, including a stretch of 33 games where no opposing runners stole a base on him. Three days after hitting his first major league home run, he caught all 19 innings of a 0-0 suspended game against the Reds at Ebbets Field in Brooklyn, the longest scoreless game in major league history.

Although the Dodgers ultimately lost the pennant to the World Series champion St. Louis Cardinals, Edwards finished strong with a .267 batting average, 13 doubles and 25 RBIs. His tremendous talent in a short amount of time also received praise, with Arthur Daley of *The New York Times* considering him perhaps the best catcher in all of baseball in the second half of the season.

1947 proved an even greater year for him, when he played in the dramatic 1947 World Series alongside Folsom native Spider Jorgensen. Starting all seven games, it was a fitting end to a season in which he hit .295, nine home runs and 80 RBIs, earning a trip to the All-Star Game and finishing fourth in balloting for the National League Most Valuable Player Award. Defensively, he led all National League catchers in chances, putouts and double plays.

For but one more signature accomplishment as a catcher, he also caught Rex Barney's no-hitter against the rival New York Giants on September 9, 1948. However, that same season saw his playing time suddenly diminish. Not only did the Dodgers call up future Hall of Famer Roy Campanella to start playing catcher, but Edwards also dealt with injury, which sadly would become a persistent issue from then on. While he would enjoy another trip to the World Series in 1949, as well as a second All-Star selection in 1951, his playing time severely decreased over the years with the Dodgers (until 1951), Chicago Cubs (1951-1952, 1954), Washington Senators (1955), and Cincinnati Reds (1956), as well as various minor league teams.

When his playing days officially ended in 1958, Edwards returned to Sacramento to work as an inventory control analyst at an aerospace firm, as well as a movie projectionist at several local theaters. He died of a heart attack on April 25, 1975, in his home in Sacramento, and is buried in the Memorial Lawn Cemetery.

14. BOB FORSCH

Born on January 13, 1950, Robert Herbert Forsch was the younger brother of fellow pitcher Ken by four years. A graduate of Hiram Johnson High School and Sacramento City College alumnus, he was drafted by the St. Louis Cardinals in the 26th round of the 1968 draft, a mere eight rounds after his older brother was selected by the Houston Astros. He was a key member of the 1982 Cardinals World Series championship squad, pitching a complete game shutout in the National League Championship Series against the Atlanta Braves. He also helped the Cardinals advance to two more World Series in 1985 and 1987, playing an especially pivotal (and confrontational) role in the 1987 National League Championship Series.

With St. Louis squaring off against the heavily favored San Francisco Giants, the teams split the first two games of the series at Busch Stadium in St. Louis before heading to Candlestick Park. Game three saw the Giants jump out to a quick 4-0 lead, thanks in part to a home run from left fielder Jeffrey Leonard. As Leonard rounded the bases, he once again displayed his "one flap down" home run trot, dropping his left arm at his side and slowly running the bases to insult St. Louis pitchers.

Entering the game to relieve starter Joe Magrane in the fourth inning, Forsch responded to this gesture in kind by hurtling a pitch right into Leonard's ribcage. The move likely galvanized the Cardinals' lifeless offense, which had been shut out in game two. They immediately scored two runs in the sixth inning and four in the seventh to take the lead for good, making Forsch the winning pitcher of the game.

Beyond his decisive postseason moments, Forsch threw not one, but two no-hitters in his career. The first came on April 16, 1978, against the Philadelphia Phillies, with the encore presentation on September 26, 1983, against the Montreal Expos. While converting from position player to pitcher before his major league career, he nonetheless distinguished himself as a solid hitter, winning Silver Slugger Awards in 1980 and 1987. Tragically, Forsch died of a sudden thoracic aortic aneurysm on November 3, 2011, mere days after throwing out the ceremonial first pitch in St. Louis before game seven of the World Series.

15. KEN FORSCH

Born in Sacramento on September 8, 1946, Kenneth Roth Forsch graduated from Hiram Johnson High School and played baseball at Oregon State University in 1967 and 1968. He was selected by the Houston Astros in the 18th round of the 1968 MLB Amateur Draft. He became one of their most reliable starting pitchers, helping them reach the postseason for the first time in franchise history in 1980. He spent the latter part of his career with the California Angels, retiring after the 1986 season.

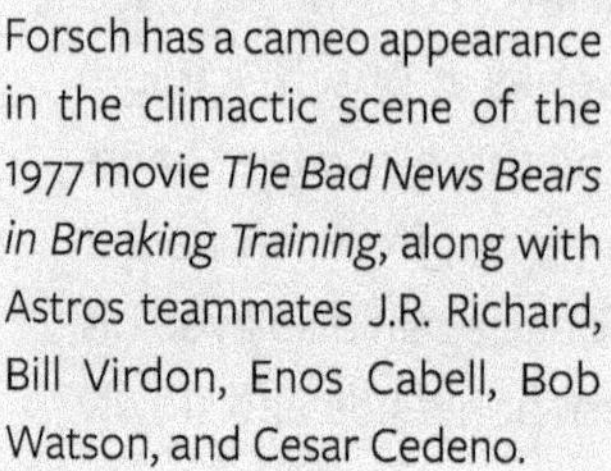

FUN FACTS

Forsch has a cameo appearance in the climactic scene of the 1977 movie *The Bad News Bears in Breaking Training*, along with Astros teammates J.R. Richard, Bill Virdon, Enos Cabell, Bob Watson, and Cesar Cedeno.

Towering on the pitcher's mound at an imposing 6' 4", Forsch was a two-time All-Star, first for the National League in 1976 with Houston and then for the American League in 1981 with the Angels. His finest moment came on April 7, 1979, when he twirled a no-hitter for Houston against the Atlanta Braves. As a result, he and Bob Forsch are the only brothers to pitch respective no-hit, no-run games in MLB history.

16. CARLOS GONZALEZ

Born in Maracaibo, Venezuela in 1985, Carlos Eduardo Gonzalez (aka "CarGo") was first signed by the Arizona Diamondbacks in August of 2002. Percolating through Arizona's minor league system over the next five years, he became one of the top prospects in all of baseball before being traded to Oakland in 2007. In 46 games with the Sacramento River Cats in 2008, he impressed with a .283 batting average and 28 RBIs. He was quickly promoted to the Athletics, making his major league debut on May 30.

Right away, Gonzalez managed an impressive feat, becoming the first player since Hall of Famer Johnny Mize in 1936 to record extra base hits as the first seven hits of his career. But in 85 total games for Oakland, he posted an underwhelming .242 batting average alongside 4 homers and 26 RBIs. After a mostly disappointing first season with the Athletics, he was traded as part of a three-player package to the Colorado Rockies for Matt Holliday that November. Spending much of the 2009 season toiling with the AAA Colorado Springs Sky Sox, a string of injuries to Colorado's outfield earned Gonzalez another call-up to the majors.

In 89 games, "CarGo" proved a muscular bat when the Rockies needed it most. Hitting .284 with 13 homers and 29 RBIs, he helped power a Rockies team that surged late in the season to reach the playoffs. Gonzalez, far from being a one-dimensional slugger, even stole 16 bases to show he had speed on the base paths. While the Rockies lost a tight National League Division Series to the defending champion Philadelphia Phillies, Gonzalez excelled even further, with 10 hits and a .588 average during the four playoff games.

This flash of potential displayed in 2009 blossomed fully in 2010, with an eye-popping .336 average, 34 home runs and 117 RBIs to win the National League batting crown and a Silver Slugger Award. He cemented his reputation as a five-tool (or as Rockies manager Jim Tracy put it, a "six-tool") player, finishing third in National League Most Valuable Player voting behind Joey Votto and Albert Pujols.

While his season numbers since haven't quite equaled his 2010 output, he's remained a stellar hitter, hitting more than 20 home runs and just below or above .300 from 2011-2013, as well as 20 or more stolen bases from 2010-2013. 2012 and 2013 also saw him earn his first All-Star selections, as well as participation in the Home Run Derby at Kauffman Stadium in 2012. Moreover, he's augmented his all-around offensive dexterity with brilliant defense in the outfield, winning Gold Glove Awards in 2010, 2012 and 2013.

17. JOE GORDON

A Los Angeles native and multi-sport athlete at the University of Oregon, Joseph Lowell Gordon first played in the Pacific Coast League as a member of the Oakland Oaks in 1936. Two years later, he donned the signature pinstripes of the New York Yankees, replacing the exalted Tony Lazzeri at second base. Gordon's rookie season in 1938 was nothing short of dazzling, slugging 25 home runs and 97 RBIs. In the 1938 World Series against the Chicago Cubs, the rookie resembled the future Hall of Famer he had replaced at second, notching a .400 batting average, a home run and 6 RBIS as New York swept Chicago for its third consecutive championship.

1939 was even more monumental, with a .284 average, 28 home runs and 111 RBIs as the Yankees secured an unprecedented fourth straight championship. While Gordon's numbers in the 1939 World Series were anemic, he would cement his October legacy in the 1941 contest against the Brooklyn Dodgers, notching .500 with a home run and 6 RBIs in New York's five-game triumph.

In terms of regular season glory, though, 1942 was his signature year. He batted .322 with 102 RBIs, while excelling defensively alongside shortstop Phil Rizzuto to create one of the best double play combos in baseball history. Even with Ted Williams' Triple Crown for the Red Sox that season, it was Gordon who received the American League Most Valuable Player Award.

After a two-year interruption of World War II service in 1944 and 1945, Gordon's average sank to .210 in the 1946 season, prompting his trade to the Cleveland Indians. "Flash" immediately bounced back, hitting .272 in 1947 with 29 home runs and 93 RBIs. Even more, his .496 slugging average trailed only Ted Williams and Joe DiMaggio. 1948, however, would prove even better. Not only did Gordon bump his offensive line to .280/32 home runs/124 RBIs in the regular season, but in doing so helped power the Indians to their first pennant and World Series championship since 1920.

Unfortunately, it marked the last peak of Gordon's playing days, as his numbers dropped precipitously in 1949 and 1950 before retirement. But his career totals in only 11 seasons were staggering: 253 home runs, 975 RBIs, nine All-Star selections (1939-1943, 1946-1949), and five World Series championships (1938, 1939, 1941, 1943, 1948). After his superb career in the majors, Gordon would call Sacramento his home in many ways. He became the manager of the Solons in 1951, in addition to playing second base for the team that season. He played as if in his prime, slashing .299 with 43 home runs and 136 RBIs, the latter two statistics being Solons club records.

That was followed by guiding the San Francisco Seals to the PCL championship in 1957, as well as scouting and managing for various MLB clubs. When his versatile tenure on the baseball diamond finally came to an end after 1969, he returned once again to Sacramento for a fruitful career in real estate. In 1974, he worked as a color commentator for the new Solons franchise in their inaugural season.

A member of the Sacramento Athletic Hall of Fame, he was later referred to by sports editor Bill Conlin as "Sacramento's best baseball player of modern times." When Gordon passed away in the River City on April 14, 1978, he remained without a plaque in the Baseball Hall of Fame. Luckily, his remarkable career would finally receive its due recognition 31 years later in 2009, when he was finally voted in by the Veterans Committee.

Gordon during his player-manager stint with the Solons. Photo courtesy of Alan O'Connor.

18. STAN HACK

Born in Sacramento in 1909, Stanley Camfield Hack is often considered the greatest baseball player to hail from the River City. After graduating from Sacramento High School, he excelled in the Sacramento Winter League. He made ends meet by working as a teller at Bank of America on 8th and J Street, and decided to take his two weeks' vacation and try out for the Solons in spring training for the 1931 season. He earned a spot on the roster as a bench player, but in April third baseman Lennie Backer took a pitch to the face. Hack was thrust into the spotlight as the starting third baseman, and he seized the moment with a .352 average and 128 runs scored that season.

Owner Lew Moreing, in need of cash, wisely sold him to the Chicago Cubs at season's end for $50,000. He would enjoy a supreme career as third baseman for the Cubs from 1932-1947. When his playing days ended, he boasted eye-popping career totals: a .301 career batting average, five All-Star selections (1938, 1939, 1941, 1943, 1945) and 2,193 hits. He had the privilege of playing in four World Series (1932, 1935, 1938, 1945), over which he hit .348. Hack also led the National League in stolen bases in 1938 and 1939, as well as hits in 1940 and 1941.

Even after passing away in 1979, Hack continues to attain extensive recognition from local and national baseball historians. John E. Spalding deemed him the greatest player to come out of Sacramento, while William Curran observed, "Hack came closest to an earthly manifestation of the ideal third baseman of the day. Tall, slender, handsome, confident – Hack was the idol of every sandlot urchin playing third base in a pair of torn knickers." While he's unsurprisingly enshrined in the Sacramento Athletic Hall of Fame, he has yet to receive a plaque at the Baseball Hall of Fame in Cooperstown, NY.

Stan Hack in a Solons uniform in 1931, the surprise breakout season that led to his sale to the Chicago Cubs. Photo courtesy of Alan O'Connor.

19. WOODIE HELD

Woodson George "Woodie" Held was born in Sacramento on March 25, 1932. Falling in love with the national pastime at age 13, Held worked three years as a batboy for the Sacramento Solons. Additionally, he spent all four years at Sacramento High School as a member of the varsity baseball team, playing every position except catcher. Following graduation, Held was scooped up by the New York Yankees, performing solidly in their minor league system and making his major league debut in September of 1954. His budding talent earned the praise of future Hall of Fame manager Casey Stengel, who opined, "He is a very good player, and I like his attitude. The ball sings when it goes off his bat...He throws as good or better than any outfielder I got."

However, "Woodie" never got the chance to make his mark in the Yankees' hallowed history, being dealt in a four-player package to the Kansas City Athletics in May of 1957. Held would ultimately notch his greatest success as a player with the Cleveland Indians, becoming the first shortstop in team history to hit at least 20 home runs in a season when he blasted 29 in 1959. He would also belt 21 in 1960, and 23 in 1961. In 1963, he was part of a historic feat, hitting the first of four consecutive Indians home runs in one inning, the first time in American League history such an event occurred.

Held was also a member of the 1966 Baltimore Orioles World Series championship team, although he didn't see any play in the Fall Classic against the Los Angeles Dodgers. All the same, he did brag that he "had the best seat in the house" for the series via the dugout. Upon retiring after the 1969 season, he finished with a career total of 179 home runs and 559 RBIs. In 2001, Held was selected as one of the 100 greatest Cleveland Indians of all-time, as part of the franchise's celebration of 100 years in the American League. He passed away at his ranch in Dubois, Wyoming on June 10, 2009, at the age of 77.

FUN FACTS

Held participated in the last games ever played at Edmonds Field in April 1964, when his Cleveland Indians played the San Francisco Giants in a pair of exhibition matches. As a Sacramento native, he was featured prominently on the official program.

20. MYRIL HOAG

Born in Davis on March 9, 1908, Myril Oliver Hoag was born with baseball in his blood. His father, Tracy Hoag, was a highly visible figure in California baseball in the early 20th century, pitching for the Stockton Millers and Santa Cruz Sand Crabs in 1908, the 1909 Fresno Raisin Growers, and the 1910 Fresno Tigers of the California League. Myril would embark on a similar path, starting in 1926 with teams in Woodland and Maxwell of the Sacramento Valley League. His efforts earned him a spot on the Sacramento Senators roster at the end of the 1926 season, becoming a regular outfielder for the club in 1929 and 1930.

After hitting an eye-popping .337 in 1930, Hoag was sold to the New York Yankees by owner Lew Moreing. He would go on to amass a sturdy major league career, patrolling the outfield for the Yankees (1931-1938), St. Louis Browns (1939-1941), Chicago White Sox (1941-1942, 1944), and Cleveland Indians (1944-1945). He was selected to the All-Star Game in 1939, a career year in which he hit .295 with 75 RBIs for the Browns.

Before that, Hoag was a member of three World Series champion-ships for the Yankees in 1932, 1937 and 1938. (He also played in the regular season for the 1936 World Series winners but saw no action in that year's Fall Classic.) The first is etched in baseball lore as the series of Babe Ruth's "called shot." In 1934, Hoag collected six hits in one game for New York, a feat not matched by another Yankee until Johnny Damon did it on June 7, 2008.

21. HARRY HOOPER

By far one of the most esteemed players with a Sacramento connection, Harry Bartholomew Hooper originally hailed from Bell Station, California. The son of a family that had migrated west for the California Gold Rush, he was given the privilege of attending school, even while his brothers had been forced to quit to help with the family farm. After high school in Oakland and a baseball tenure at Saint Mary's College of California (where he also received an engineering degree), he started his minor league career with the Oakland Commuters in 1907. Converting from pitcher to position player, Hooper batted .301 in 156 at-bats.

1908 saw him suit up for the Sacramento Senators, hitting .344 in 77 games. Hooper's contract with the team even secured him financially off the field, providing work as a railroad surveyor. Far from a mere minor league pitstop, Hooper's time with Sacramento, unbeknownst to him, would be his direct path to the major leagues. The Senators' manager, Charles Graham, also worked as a scout for the Boston Red Sox, and quickly arranged a meeting between Hooper and Red Sox owner John I. Taylor. He signed a $2,850 contract to play for Boston and proved a worthy investment right away in 1909, with a .282 average and impeccable defense in right field.

The 1910s saw Hooper carve a hallowed place in baseball history, teaming up with centerfielder Tris Speaker and left fielder Duffy Lewis to form one of the greatest outfields the game has ever witnessed. Throughout the decade, the "Million Dollar Outfield" combined for 445 assists, of which Hooper accounted for 150. In 1910, Hooper played 155 games and led the league with 688 plate appearances, while leading American League outfielders with 30 assists. 1911 was even more stellar, hitting .311 (giving the outfield a combined average of .315 that season). In 1912, his average dipped to .242, but he would provide enough heroics that season with his glove.

In the final game of the 1912 World Series, with Boston facing the New York Giants, Hooper made a spectacular barehanded catch to rob Larry Doyle of a home run and preserve Boston's championship. A deeply religious man, he was said to have prayed for a victory beforehand, thus attributing his improbable catch to divine intervention. In 1913, he achieved the rare feat of hitting a home run to lead off both games of a doubleheader.

After 230 putouts in the outfield in 1914, Hooper reprised his role as a World Series hero in 1915, hitting two home runs in game five to cement Boston's second championship of the decade. He helped them win two more titles in 1916 and 1918, certifying that decade's Boston teams as among the most dominant in baseball history. Throughout his tenure in Boston, he endeared himself to fans, teammates and opposing players with his affable personality and humor as well as his consummate talent, a stark contrast to the stoic demeanor of his outfield companion Speaker.

According to Hooper's recollections to writer Lawrence Ritter, he even helped set another chapter of baseball history in motion in 1919. As the newly minted team captain, he convinced Red Sox manager Ed Barrow to start playing pitcher Babe Ruth in the outfield when Ruth wasn't on the mound. As Hooper astutely observed, Ruth possessed powerful hitting skills and massive crowd appeal as well as pitching finesse. Of course, Ruth's game-changing outbreak as a slugger would happen after Boston owner Harry Frazee ignominiously sold him to the rival New York Yankees following the 1919 season.

Hooper was consigned to the same fate in March of 1921, being traded to the Chicago White Sox. Despite initial threats to retire after salary disagreements with Chicago owner Charles Comiskey, Hooper flourished in a White Sox uniform, hitting over .300 in three of his five seasons there and reaching double digits in season home run tallies for the first time. When he left the White Sox in 1925 to pursue a career as a manager, his major league career totals came to an incredible .281 average, 2,466 hits, 816 RBIs, 160 triples, and 375 stolen bases, as well as four World Series championships.

After a stint as manager of the San Francisco Missions of the Pacific Coast League, he worked in real estate and as the postmaster of Capitola, CA for 24 years starting in 1933. He remained busy all throughout his later life, taking up hunting and fishing in addition to faithfully following his former Red Sox and the San Francisco Giants. Hooper would finally be elected to the Baseball Hall of Fame in 1971, three years prior to his death in Santa Cruz, CA.

22. J.P. HOWELL

Originally from Modesto, James Phillip Howell attended St. Mary's School in Sacramento. An alumnus of Jesuit High School in Carmichael too, he helped lead the Texas Longhorns to the final round of the 2004 College World Series, notching a 0.77 ERA throughout the tournament. He made his major league debut with the Kansas City Royals the following year, before being traded to the Tampa Bay Devil Rays. Originally pegged as a starting pitcher, he was moved from the rotation to the bullpen for the 2008 season, much to his benefit and the team's.

Newly minted as the Tampa Bay Rays, the club shocked the sports world with a 97-65 regular season record and an American League East Division title. Howell excelled likewise with a pristine 6-1 record and 2.22 ERA as the Rays reached their first World Series in franchise history. After missing the entire 2010 season due to a torn labrum, he rebounded to help the Rays reach the postseason again in 2011 in a thrilling late-season push.

Despite trailing the Boston Red Sox by nine games on September 1, Tampa Bay rallied to clinch a playoff spot over them in the final game of the regular season, beating the Yankees on a walk-off homer in the 12th inning to cap off what some regard as the greatest all-around day in MLB regular season history. Howell did his part throughout September, pitching in ten games with four holds and giving up runs only once.

After Tampa Bay, Howell subsequently played a key part in the Los Angeles Dodgers bullpen, helping the team win four consecutive division titles from 2013 to 2016, two of which (2013 and 2014) were alongside fellow Sacramentan Brandon League. Howell was even the winning pitcher in the team's come-from-behind 7-6 win to clinch in Arizona on September 19, 2013. He has recently continued his professional baseball career by pitching for the independent San Rafael Pacifics.

23. GEOFF JENKINS

Originally from Olympia, Washington, Geoff Jenkins attended Cordova High School in Rancho Cordova. Excelling as a multi-sport athlete, Jenkins was selected to the all-state baseball team as a junior and senior before graduating in 1992. He continued to succeed in college baseball at USC, earning numerous awards and honors and helping them reach the College World Series in 1995. He later played the majority of his MLB career for the Milwaukee Brewers, with a powerful bat that earned him a trip to the All-Star Game in 2003.

He finished his career as a member of the 2008 Philadelphia Phillies World Series championship team, socking a leadoff double in the bottom of the sixth inning of game five that helped Philadelphia capture its first title in 28 years. His 221 career home runs (212 of them with Milwaukee) rank fourth all-time in Brewers franchise history, trailing only Robin Yount, Ryan Braun and Prince Fielder. Jenkins was inducted into the Sacramento Sports Hall of Fame in 2019.

24. NICK JOHNSON

Born in Sacramento on September 19, 1978, Nicholas Robert Johnson was born with a blood connection to one of the city's most esteemed baseball figures, Larry Bowa. As Bowa's nephew, Johnson followed in his footsteps by attending C.K. McClatchy High School before being drafted by the New York Yankees in 1996. Debuting in late 2001, he donned Yankee pinstripes as a first baseman and designated hitter for two full seasons, including a trip to the World Series in 2003 (a season in which he hit .284 with 14 home runs and 47 RBIs while playing in 96 games). Before the 2004 season, he was traded to the Montreal Expos, the team's last before their relocation to Washington, D.C.

While his 2004 campaign was significantly stunted by injury, he excelled in the franchise's first season as the Washington Nationals the very next year, hitting .289 with 15 home runs and 74 RBIs. He did even better in 2006, managing a .290/23/77 line. However, a broken femur sustained on a collision in September of 2006 caused him to miss the entire 2007 season, and the remaining years of his career continued to be riddled with frequent injury.

Nonetheless, Johnson enjoyed some notable highlights even as his playing time was limited. When he was traded from Washington to the Florida Marlins in July of 2009, he was the team's last player to have also suited up as a Montreal Expo. In the 2009 season, his .426 on-base percentage was second in the league behind sure-to-be Hall of Famer Albert Pujols.

This was a testament to Johnson's exceptional patience and discipline at the plate, leading him to have a career on-base percentage of .399. He was also notably prolific throughout his career with the bases loaded, hitting .370 with 72 RBIs and 2 grand slams in that situation. He retired in January of 2013, ending a strong career whose full potential was unfortunately stifled by many injuries.

25. NIPPY JONES

Born in Los Angeles on June 29, 1925, Vernal "Nippy" Jones first took the field for the Solons as a first and second baseman during their disastrous 1943 campaign. However, like many baseball stars at the time, his career was temporarily interrupted by World War II service, serving in the Marine Corps from 1943 to 1946. He returned to baseball in 1946 with the Rochester Red Wings, batting a muscular .344 that season. However, he lost the International League batting title to a certain fellow named Jackie Robinson, who hit .349. His performance earned him a late-season call-up to the St. Louis Cardinals, batting .333 in 16 games and even making a brief appearance in the team's thrilling World Series victory against the Boston Red Sox.

However, his affiliation with Sacramento baseball didn't end when he went to the major leagues. After spending most of the 1952 season in the Phillies' minor league system, he returned to play for the Solons until 1957. During this stretch, he averaged .298 at the plate and enjoyed great popularity among Solons fans. So much, in fact, that *Sacramento Bee* sports editor Bill Conlin wrote he might have been the most popular player in all of Sacramento.

Immediately following his fruitful stint with the Solons, Nippy contributed to the Milwaukee Braves' 1957 World Series title, albeit in an absurd way. In the bottom of the 10th inning of game four at Milwaukee County Stadium, the Yankees led 5-4, and were three outs away from taking a 3-1 lead in the series. Jones, pinch-hitting for pitcher Warren Spahn, led off the inning against Yankees pitcher Tommy Byrne. The first pitch to Jones bounced in the dirt, and home plate umpire Augie Donatelli called it ball one.

However, Nippy insisted the pitch had actually hit his foot, and immediately proffered the ball, indicating a smudge of shoe polish as the evidence. He was thusly awarded first base, kickstarting a game-winning rally that culminated with slugger Eddie Mathews' game-winning two-run homer. This moment has forever been etched in baseball history as the "Shoeshine Incident," by far one of the funniest and strangest occurrences in World Series history.

Jones receiving a fresh coat of black shoe polish from Braves equipment manager Joe Taylor before game five of the 1957 World Series. It was that very substance that proved the difference between victory and defeat in the prior game. Photo courtesy of Alan O'Connor.

After another quick spell with the Solons, Jones retired from baseball in 1960. He worked in public relations and title insurance in Sacramento thereafter, before becoming a professional fishing guide on the Sacramento River. He died of a heart attack on October 3, 1995, and is buried in Southeast Lawn Memorial Park.

26. SPIDER JORGENSEN

Born in Folsom on November 3, 1919, John Donald "Spider" Jorgensen was the son of a father who worked as a dredge operator on the Sacramento River Delta and a mother who was the daughter of Irish immigrants. He attended Folsom High School, graduating in 1936 and even earning his famous nickname there. Strangely, he earned it not while playing baseball, but basketball.

While shooting hoops with other students at school, Jorgensen wore a pair of black shorts with an orange stripe. A teacher passing by, who had recently cleaned out a woodshed with a black widow spider in it, said Jorgensen's attire reminded him of the spider. After high school, he attended Sacramento City College in 1937 and 1938, followed by a couple years of odd jobs and playing baseball around the city (including the Sacramento Winter League).

In 1940, his fortunes changed with a successful tryout for the Brooklyn Dodgers at a training camp in San Mateo, CA. He signed a contract with the club and immediately advanced to their Santa Barbara team in the Class C California League. Jorgensen proved an instant success in his first pro season in 1941, batting .332 with nine home runs and 43 doubles to earn league Most Valuable Player. However, the Japanese attack on Pearl Harbor later that year ushered America's entry into World War II, and Jorgensen answered the call of duty with four years of service in the Army Air Corps.

Following his discharge in 1945, he returned to the Dodgers organization the next year with their AAA club in the International League, the Montreal Royals. Hitting .293 in 117 games that year, Spider shared the infield diamond with none other than Jackie Robinson, the rising superstar on track to break Major League Baseball's color barrier. After injuries to infielders Cookie Lavagetto and Arky Vaughan before the 1947 season, Jorgensen found himself the starting third baseman. His rookie debut would coincide with one of the most important moments in American history.

It was April 15, 1947, the same day Robinson broke baseball's color barrier for the Dodgers, and Brooklyn's civil rights hero was more than willing to help out his fellow rookie. Recalled Jorgensen: "I came into Ebbets Field on Opening Day, scared to death. I didn't think I was going to play. I didn't have any equipment on me. My glove, bats, everything else went to Syracuse because the Montreal club opened up there. Then Jackie comes over and says, 'Here, use my second base glove.' He was going to play first base. So I used his glove and borrowed a pair of spikes, and I'm in the lineup. So I really didn't have time to get nervous."

He managed a walk and an RBI in Brooklyn's 5-3 victory over the Boston Braves, kicking off an indelible year for himself and the team. Jorgensen would hit .274 as Brooklyn's regular third baseman, with 29 doubles and eight triples, as the Dodgers won their first National League pennant in six years. Deemed the "best of the hot corner rookies" by Dan Daniel of *The Sporting News*, he played in all seven games of Brooklyn's World Series loss against the New York Yankees, with four hits and three RBIs in what is often considered one of the best Fall Classics ever played.

Unfortunately, Jorgensen would never be quite the same player after the storybook year of 1947, as he permanently damaged his arm by throwing too hard during the next spring training. His throwing arm also sustained damage from rifle recoil while hunting. While still managing to hit .300 in limited action in 1948, he was never the same player, playing only 107 games after that year with the Dodgers and New York Giants until 1951. After the majors, Jorgensen spent several years playing with the Oakland Oaks of the Pacific Coast League. He eventually returned to Sacramento in 1962, putting his skills to work as an amateur baseball coach.

Most prominently, he was head coach of the Fair Oaks American Legion team, who won the Legion North Division championship in 1967. Among his players was a teenaged Dusty Baker, who was impressed by Jorgensen's humility. In the 2004 book *How To Be Like Jackie Robinson*, Baker recalled, "In all the time he coached us, I never knew Spider played for the Dodgers. I knew he was a terrific coach, but he never once mentioned he was a former player."

For the next few decades, Jorgensen also excelled as a major league scout for various teams, discovering and advocating for talented play-ers such as Bob Walk and Mark Grace. In 1996, he was in the first class of inductees for the Sacramento City College Athletic Hall of Fame. He's also portrayed in the 2013 film *42* by actor Jamie Ruehling. Jorgensen passed away on November 6, 2003, in Rancho Cucamonga, CA.

Jorgensen during his time with the New York Giants. Photo courtesy of Alan O'Connor.

27. BRANDON LEAGUE

Born in Sacramento in 1983, League was drafted out of Saint Louis School in Honolulu, Hawaii by the Toronto Blue Jays in 2001. He worked as a relief pitcher for the Blue Jays, Seattle Mariners and Los Angeles Dodgers. As Seattle's closer, he was selected to the All-Star Game in 2011, finishing the season with a 2.79 ERA and 37 saves. His most distinguished moment came on June 8, 2012, when he combined with Seattle starter Kevin Millwood and fellow relievers Charlie Furbush, Stephen Pryor, Lucas Luetge, and Tom Wilhelmsen to pitch a combined no-hitter against the Dodgers. He also contributed to consecutive Dodgers National League West Division titles in 2013 and 2014.

28. DERREK LEE

Born in Sacramento in 1975, Derrek Leon Lee played locally for Whitney Little League before graduating from El Camino High School in 1993. He amassed an excellent career as a first baseman from 1997-2011 with the San Diego Padres, Florida Marlins, Chicago Cubs, Atlanta Braves, Baltimore Orioles, and Pittsburgh Pirates. A member of the 2003 Marlins World Series championship team, Lee roped a game-tying double in the eighth inning of game six of the NLCS against the Cubs, aiding Florida's comeback win in what is best known as the "Steve Bartman Game." He would later help the Cubs reach the playoffs in 2007 and 2008, and the Braves in 2010.

His individual achievements include two All-Star selections (2005, 2007), three Gold Glove Awards (2003, 2005, 2007), and a Silver Slugger Award and the National League batting crown in 2005 thanks to his .335 batting average. Retiring after the 2011 season, Lee finished with a stellar career line that includes a .281 batting average, 331 home runs and 1,078 RBIs. Lee's accomplishments were recognized with induction into the Sacramento Sports Hall of Fame in 2017.

29. BRAD LIDGE

Born in Sacramento on December 23, 1976, Bradley Thomas Lidge grew up playing baseball, basketball and football in Colorado. Attending Notre Dame for college, he embarked on a sometimes turbulent, but ultimately triumphant, major league career. Debuting with the Houston Astros in 2002, Lidge quickly became one of the team's star relief pitchers. In 2003, he was the winning pitcher of Houston's combined no-hitter against the New York Yankees on June 11 (the other pitchers being Roy Oswalt, Pete Munro, Kirk Saarloos, Octavio Dotel, and Billy Wagner). In 2004, his 157 strikeouts set the National League record for strikeouts by a reliever in a single season.

2005 saw Lidge attain even greater heights, but also painful defeat. With 42 saves and a pristine 2.29 ERA in the regular season, he easily earned his first All-Star selection. The playoffs, however, proved a cruel setback. With Houston one out away from clinching their first National League pennant at home in game five of the National League Championship Series, Lidge surrendered a towering three-run homer to St. Louis Cardinals slugger Albert Pujols, which ultimately forced a sixth game.

While the Astros rebounded to win the pennant the next game, they were swept in the World Series by the Chicago White Sox, with Lidge giving up a walk-off home run in game two and the series-clinching hit in game four. For the next two years, many believed he'd never be the same dominant closer as before. In 2008, he found the ultimate redemption as a member of the Philadelphia Phillies World Series championship team, notching a "perfect season" where he converted every single save opportunity in the regular season and playoffs (including the last out of the World Series).

As a result of this impeccable season, Lidge won National League Comeback Player of the Year and National League Rolaids Relief Man of the Year for 2008, in addition to a second All-Star selection. Following that, Lidge was a member of three more Phillies postseason teams in 2009, 2010 and 2011, helping the club reach a second consecutive World Series in 2009. He retired from baseball after a brief stint with the Washington Nationals in 2012 and has since dedicated himself to studying archaeology in Europe.

30. JERRY MANUEL

A native of Hahira, Georgia, Manuel attended Cordova High School in Rancho Cordova. After a brief playing career that lasted from 1975 to 1982 for the Detroit Tigers, Montreal Expos and San Diego Padres, he made his greatest mark as a coach and manager. First serving as a coach for the Expos from 1991 to 1996, he worked as bench coach under Jim Leyland for the 1997 World Series champion Florida Marlins. This was followed by five years as manager of the Chicago White Sox, during which he won 2000 American League Manager of the Year for guiding the team to 95 wins and an American League Central Division title.

Following his time in Chicago, he worked as a coach for the New York Mets from 2005 until manager Willie Randolph was fired in June 2008. From then through the end of the 2010 season, Manuel served as manager of the Mets. His post-baseball activities have included working as an analyst for MLB Network, as well as Director of Baseball Operations at William Jessup University in Rocklin, CA.

31. PEPPER MARTIN

Born in Temple, Oklahoma in 1904, Johnny Leonard Roosevelt "Pepper" Martin is best known as one of the integral members of the 1930s St. Louis Cardinals. Buoyed by an eccentric core of talented players such as Dizzy Dean, Leo Durocher and Spud Davis, the team was famously dubbed the "Gashouse Gang" for their scrappy playing style, on-field antics and unkempt appearance. As a third baseman and outfielder, Martin earned four All-Star selections (1933, 1934, 1935, 1937) and fueled the Cardinals' 1931 and 1934 World Series championship teams.

His performance in the 1931 World Series in particular is one of the most storied individual efforts in the history of the Fall Classic, batting .500 with 5 RBIs, a home run, four doubles, and clutch defensive heroics to lead St. Louis to an upset victory over the heavily favored Philadelphia Athletics. Whether in an early season game or with a championship on the line, Martin played every moment with an intense vivacity that led some to label him the next Ty

Cobb. Ultimately, this hustling, exuberant style of play took a physical toll on his body, and as a result, "Pepper" never quite lived up to the full potential many felt he possessed.

However, this somewhat abrupt decline and departure from the majors prefaced Martin's storied triumph in Sacramento. He immediately became the manager of the Solons for the 1941 season, in which they amassed a 102-75 record. 1942 witnessed even greater fortunes, with a 105-73 record and the Solons' exhilarating Pacific Coast League championship at the end of the season. It was the first PCL crown in franchise history, and the last by any team in the city until 2003. After officially retiring as a player with the Cardinals in 1944, Martin spent most of his remaining years as a minor league manager in the South before dying of a heart attack in 1965.

Martin in the dugout during the Solons' storybook 1942 season. Photo courtesy of Alan O'Connor.

32. BUCK MARTINEZ

Born in Redding, California, John Albert "Buck" Martinez first displayed his baseball prowess at Elk Grove High School. An all-conference catcher for three years, he capped off his time there with a .512 average in his senior year. After that was a stint at Sacramento City College, helping the school team reach two consecutive state championship games, before finishing his education at Sacramento State University.

Martinez (center, crouching) poses with SCC Panthers teammates Al Simas (holding umbrella) and Ken Hottman (holding bat) in 1967. Photo courtesy of the Sac City Express.

Martinez debuted as a major league catcher with the Kansas City Royals in 1969, the first year the franchise took the field. Despite gaining a reputation as a hitter of limited skill, he nonetheless hit .333 with 4 RBIs in the 1976 American League Championship Series against the Yankees, widely considered one of the best in playoff history. After his time with the Royals ended in 1977, he spent three seasons with the Milwaukee Brewers before making his biggest mark as a catcher for the Toronto Blue Jays from 1981-1986.

In addition to improving his offensive skills, Martinez earned recognition as an excellent defensive catcher. This reputation was encapsulated by a particularly brutal moment on July 9, 1985, against the Seattle Mariners. Gorman Thomas, Martinez's former teammate in Milwaukee, roped a single to right field with runner Phil Bradley on second. Blue Jays outfielder Jesse Barfield fired the ball to Martinez at home, who caught it and tagged Bradley for the out. However, Bradley slid into Martinez so hard he broke the catcher's leg and dislocated his ankle.

Even then, he gathered himself enough to try and throw out Thomas at third base, but his throw sailed into left field. With Thomas heading to home plate, outfielder George Bell scooped it up and threw it back to Martinez, who managed to catch it even as he remained sprawled on his back. Thomas, seeing his friend and former teammate in pain, eased up as he came home, allowing Martinez to tag him out and complete the only 9-2-7-2 double play in MLB history.

While maintaining a humble attitude about his pain-defying heroics to this day, he won the admiration of many, with Toronto manager Jimy Williams deeming it the greatest play he'd ever seen. In his book *From Worst to First: The Toronto Blue Jays in 1985*, Martinez curtly stated, "It was not an unusual play, at least for me. I was just blocking the plate, trying to save a run in a scoreless tie. Nothing heroic." As a result of the injuries he sustained, Martinez not only missed playing in Toronto's first ever postseason that year but was effectively finished as a player. He attempted a brief comeback in 1986 before officially retiring after hitting a mere .181 in 81 games.

Since retirement, Martinez has enjoyed a rewarding career as a commentator and radio host. Starting as a color analyst for the Canadian channel The Sports Network in 1987, he would eventually move up to ESPN telecasts, as well as lending his voice to EA Sports' popular *Triple Play Baseball* video games. In the 2000s, Martinez added Baltimore Orioles color commentator, co-host of XM Radio's *Baseball This Morning*, and Sunday afternoon game and postseason commentator for TBS to his broadcasting resume. Martinez has also done his share of coaching, managing the U.S. team in the first ever World Baseball Classic in 2006 (whose roster included Sacramento native Derrek Lee). As of this publication, he's working as the play-by-play announcer of the Blue Jays.

33. JOE MARTY

One of Sacramento baseball's most cherished figures, Joseph Anton Marty was born on September 1, 1913, at 522 M St. A multifaceted sports star at Christian Brothers High School, he graduated in 1931 and attended St. Mary's College in Moraga, CA. Attending on a sports scholarship, he continued to excel in baseball, football and basketball.

Of the three major sports, it was baseball that proved his calling. He went on to become one of the best Pacific Coast League hitters of the '30s, winning the league batting crown in 1936 while playing for the San Francisco Seals. He even played in the same outfield as fellow Northern California native and future Yankees Hall of Fame legend Joe DiMaggio.

After his storied time in the PCL, Marty amassed a brief tenure in the majors with the Chicago Cubs (1937-1939) and Philadelphia Phillies (1939-1941). 1938 in Chicago was by far his most unforgettable year in the major leagues. Not only did he play with fellow Sacramento native Stan Hack as a teammate, but he hit .500 with a home run against the Yankees in that year's World Series. When his home run cleared the left field fence at Yankee Stadium in game three, he became the first Sacramento native ever to hit one in the Fall Classic.

His performance in the 1938 World Series wasn't his only highlight that year. He also opened his namesake bar on J Street, but his business and baseball duties were interrupted by four years of service in World War II. Upon returning from the war, he suited up for his hometown Sacramento Solons from 1946 to 1952, even serving as manager for the second half of the 1950 season.

After the 1952 season, Marty retired from the game to focus solely on tending to his bar, which had been moved from J Street to 15th & Broadway in 1951. With its proximity to Edmonds Field a few blocks away, it enjoyed even greater business. Marty tended the bar all the way until his death on October 4, 1984.

The bar continued to operate until it was destroyed by a fire in 2005. Fortunately, under the ownership of Sampino's Kitchen, Joe Marty's was relaunched in 2015 and continues to live on at its old location on Broadway today. Right next to the Tower Theater and Café, its humble baseball neon sign glows brightly, inviting passersby to relish Marty's legacy and that of Sacramento baseball.

Joe Marty's restaurant as it looks today on Broadway, next to the Tower Theater and Café. Photo taken by Morgan Garvey.

34. JOHN MCNAMARA

Born in Sacramento in 1932, John Francis McNamara attended Christian Brothers High School and Sacramento Junior College (now Sacramento City College). In 1951, as team captain of the SJC Panthers, McNamara led the team to a 29-3 season record and the first state baseball championship in school history. He immediately advanced to the minor leagues as a catcher, beginning in 1951 with the Fresno Cardinals of the California League. Over the next 18 years, he took the field for a multitude of minor league teams, including 76 games with the Solons in 1956.

McNamara while playing with the 1956 Sacramento Solons. Photo courtesy of Alan O'Connor.

When his playing days ended in the late '60s, he moved on to a successful career as a major league coach and manager for the next 20 years. Starting as a coach for the Oakland Athletics in 1968, he became manager late in 1969 upon Hank Bauer's firing. McNamara led the club to an outstanding 89-73 record in 1970, yet found himself under the managerial axe following the season. It wasn't due to his lack of competence as manager; Oakland's eccentric owner, Charles O. Finley, frequently fired managers even in times of success. McNamara's coaching and managerial influence on the club would pay off two years later, when the A's won the first of three consecutive World Series titles.

Following his firing in Oakland, McNamara imparted his baseball skills across the bay as the third base coach for the San Francisco Giants from 1971 to 1973, where he struck a unique relationship with superstar Willie Mays. The future Hall of Famer, despite a reputation as the most skilled five-tool player of all-time, had a notorious habit of ignoring his third base coach. McNamara asked Mays to trust his judgment on whether or not he could outrun the throw of a particular opposing outfielder. Mays did so, making McNamara the only third base coach he ever trusted in his storied 22-year career. After his tenure coaching Mays and the Giants (including a trip to the playoffs in 1971), McNamara assumed the managerial reigns of the San Diego Padres from 1974 to 1977.

Following that with a year of coaching the California Angels in 1978, he managed the Cincinnati Reds to the postseason in 1979, although his 1981 Reds were denied a trip to the playoffs due to the split-season format of the strike-shortened season. This was despite the fact that the Reds had the best combined record in the National League West of both half-seasons, leading many Reds fans to famously declare, "We Wuz Robbed!" Following his time managing the Reds and then the Angels in 1983 and 1984, McNamara experienced his greatest fortunes with the Boston Red Sox from 1985 to 1988.

The 1986 season saw Boston storm to a 95-66 record, earning the American League East Division crown and a berth in the American League Championship Series against the Angels. After falling behind three games to one, Boston mounted an incredible comeback win in game five thanks to Dave Henderson's two-strike, two-out home run in the top of the ninth inning. They proceeded to win games six and seven in Boston in resounding fashion, advancing to their first World Series since 1975.

While the Red Sox fell in a heartbreaking World Series against the New York Mets, McNamara still earned recognition by winning 1986 American League Manager of the Year. However, he was fired midway through the 1988 season, and followed it up with a subpar 1990 season managing Cleveland before being fired halfway through again in 1991. He ended his managerial career with interim stints with the Angels in 1996 and 1997.

35. EARL MCNEELY

Born in Sacramento in 1898, Earl George McNeely distinguished himself early in life as an excellent all-around athlete, playing basketball and soccer locally. Interestingly, he didn't even take up baseball until returning from service in World War I, playing in the National Division of the Sacramento Winter League. Sacramento Senators owner Lew Moreing was quick to spot his versatility, which he displayed by playing second base, third base and outfield for the Senators from 1922-1924.

Quickly gaining recognition for his incredible speed, McNeely earned a deal with the major league Washington Senators in 1924. Debuting that season on August 9, McNeely would end up being a key player in a historic run. The Senators had long been derided as one of the most anemic teams in the American League, inspiring the phrase: "Washington - first in war, first in peace, and last in the American League." But under the guidance of their "boy wonder" 27-year-old player-manager, future Hall of Famer Bucky Harris, the Senators finally won the AL pennant, facing the New York Giants in the World Series.

The series was a back-and-forth affair that culminated in a winner-take-all game seven at Griffith Stadium in Washington, D.C. After Washington rallied to tie the game 3-3 in the eighth inning on a clutch hit from Harris, the game extended into the 12th inning thanks to the relief efforts of future Hall of Famer Walter "Big Train" Johnson (who was primarily a starting pitcher). In the bottom of the 12th, with Muddy Ruel representing the winning run at second base and Johnson at first, McNeely stepped to the plate with a chance to be the hero.

He proceeded to lace a hit towards Giants third baseman Freddie Lindstrom, but the ball hit a pebble in the dirt and took a bizarre hop over

Lindstrom's head. The ball sailed into the outfield, scoring Ruel and giving Washington the victory in what has since been universally hailed as one of the greatest World Series ever played. In a truly bizarre twist, it was exactly the same as Harris's game-tying RBI hit in the eighth, which also took a bounce over Lindstrom's head.

McNeely followed his October heroics of 1924 with a stellar 1925 season, hitting .286 in 122 games as the Senators repeated as American League champions. However, they lost a heartbreaking World Series to the Pittsburgh Pirates, and McNeely's fortunes as a ballplayer would decline precipitously thereafter. He managed a .303 average in 1926, but a drop in average in 1927 factored into the Senators sending him to the St. Louis Brown before the 1928 season, playing for them through 1931 before retiring from the major leagues. While his diminishing skills and average forced him out of the majors relatively quickly, McNeely still had a prosperous life and career in his hometown to look forward to.

Returning to the Sacramento Senators in 1932, he became their manager that same year, continuing as a player-manager until 1934. While he enjoyed renewed success as player, in addition to an above .500 winning percentage as manager, the Senators organization fell into financial hardship in 1934 when owner Lew Moreing failed to make his loan payments on the team. A group of local banks assumed ownership of the club and tapped McNeely to be the de facto team president. But their dismal results in the 1935 season led to the franchise's purchase by the St. Louis Cardinals, after which he was dismissed altogether.

After two years of coaching the Washington Senators in 1936 and 1937, he returned to settle in Orangevale and pursued a variety of jobs and community projects such as investment, real estate and farming. In an interesting parallel to another Sacramento baseball figure, Butch Metzger, McNeely was also heavily involved with local fire departments, serving as a volunteer and director for Orangevale and Citrus Heights departments before becoming the first president of the Sacramento County Fire Directors Association.

His other community involvements included trustee for Orangevale Elementary Schools and American River College and president of the Sacramento County Fair board of directors. An inductee in the Sacramento Athletic Hall of Fame, he died in Sacramento on July 16, 1971, at the age of 73.

McNeely with Sacramento in 1932, the year he returned to the team after his prime years in the majors. Photo courtesy of Alan O'Connor.

36. BUTCH METZGER

Born in Lafayette, Indiana in 1952, Clarence Edward "Butch" Metzger played baseball at John F. Kennedy High School in Sacramento. He was drafted by the San Francisco Giants in the second round of the 1970 amateur draft, debuting as a relief pitcher with them in September of 1974. While he managed a 3.55 ERA in a limited number of innings, he was traded in the offseason to the San Diego Padres. His 1975 season was limited due to control issues, with four walks and a 7.71 ERA in only 4.2 innings pitched that year.

In 1976, Metzger finally smoothened out his control and enjoyed an excellent season. He finished the year with an 11-4 record, a 2.92 ERA, 89 strikeouts, 16 saves, and a league-leading 62 games finished. For his remarkable improvement in more playing time, he was voted co-National League Rookie of the Year alongside Cincinnati Reds pitcher Pat Zachry.

However, Metzger only played two more full seasons in the majors, finishing with the New York Mets in 1978. After the Mets, he tumbled down the baseball ladder to the AAA Oklahoma City 89ers, then to Caracas, Venezuela in the Inter-American League (a league that became defunct soon thereafter), and finally to a minor league club in Richmond, Virginia.

He quit baseball at a coach's insistence and worked as a warehouse painter, while still craving the adrenaline rush that the sport provided. A few years later, Metzger would provide relief once again in high-stakes situations, albeit in the far more important capacity as a fireman for West Sacramento Fire Station No. 1.

Despite the disparity in real life stakes, relief pitching proved a fitting antecedent to firefighting. In his words, "Going to a fire is like the phone ringing in the bullpen and the hair on the back of your neck standing up. Going to a fire is like, 'Give me the ball.'...You know like what happened on my first few fires? I get there and I'm thinking, 'Hey, I've been here before.'"

37. MARK MULDER

Originally hailing from South Holland, Illinois, Mark Alan Mulder displayed a penchant for sports from an incredibly young age. He quickly showed a restless interest in baseball, basketball, soccer, golf, and water-skiing. Baseball earned Mulder's strongest affinity, playing T-Ball and Little League and growing up idolizing Chicago White Sox slugger Harold Baines. At Thornwood

High School in South Holland, he helped the team gain national recognition from the likes of *USA Today*, distinguishing himself as both a powerful hitter and a crafty left-handed pitcher. Not to mention, he was quite imposing to face in either position thanks to his towering 6' 6" height.

Mulder would go on to develop his skills in the latter capacity for the Michigan State Spartans, gaining the attention of Billy Beane and the Oakland Athletics at the 1998 MLB Amateur Draft. After being selected, he immediately excelled with the AAA Vancouver Canadians in 1999, right before the franchise was purchased by Art Savage and moved to Sacramento. Like fellow ace Barry Zito, Mulder's time as a River Cat in their inaugural 2000 season was abbreviated by a promotion to the Athletics. Unlike Zito, he didn't enjoy an impeccable start to his major league career, going 9-10 with a 5.44 ERA.

Fortunately, it proved only a temporary stumble on the road to being one of Oakland's aces the following year in 2001, totaling a league-leading 21 wins and four shutouts to finish second in voting for the American League Cy Young Award to Roger Clemens. Mulder continued to shine for the next three seasons in an A's uniform, earning All-Star selections in 2003 and 2004 and leading the league in complete games both seasons. After a trade to the St. Louis Cardinals before the 2005 season, he enjoyed a terrific start in the National League, with a 16-8 record and a 3.64 ERA as the Cardinals advanced to the second round of the playoffs.

2006, however, proved a grim one for Mulder. While St. Louis would win their first World Series in 24 years, Mulder's season was ended by rotator cuff and shoulder injuries. He continued to be stunted by injuries over the next few seasons, effectively retiring in 2010. Mulder attempted a comeback with the Los Angeles Angels of Anaheim in 2014, but unfortunately suffered a torn Achilles tendon during agility drills in spring training. Since retirement, he's worked primarily as an analyst for ESPN's *Baseball Tonight* and Athletics broadcasts.

38. DARREN OLIVER

Born in Kansas City, Missouri, Darren Christopher Oliver played baseball and basketball at Rio Linda High School. He was selected to the All-City team in 1988, the same year the Texas Rangers drafted him. Oliver's accomplished MLB career spanned two decades in the majors as a starting and relief pitcher from 1993 to 2013, suiting up for the Rangers, St. Louis Cardinals, Boston Red Sox, Colorado Rockies, Florida Marlins, Houston Astros, New York Mets, Los Angeles Angels of Anaheim, and Toronto Blue Jays.

He finished with a career win-loss record of 118-98, 1,259 strikeouts and numerous playoff appearances, including consecutive trips to the World Series with Texas in 2010 and 2011. He was also the winning pitcher in the Angels' series-clinching come-from-behind win in game three of the 2009 ALDS in Boston.

In the regular season, Oliver was a key player in two baseball milestones. On June 12, 1997, he became the first pitcher to partake in interleague play, starting for the Rangers in a 4-3 loss to the San Francisco Giants at the Ballpark in Arlington. A year later, pitching for the Cardinals, he was the starting and winning pitcher in the game where Mark McGwire hit his record-tying 61st home run on September 7, 1998.

39. DUSTIN PEDROIA

A Woodland native, Dustin Pedroia displayed his prodigious baseball talent first at Woodland High School, batting .445 in his senior year and not striking out even once. After excelling in college at Arizona State University, he was drafted in the second round of the 2004 MLB Draft by the Boston Red Sox. As second baseman for Boston from 2006 to present, Pedroia has been hailed as one of the best in the position throughout all of Major League Baseball. As of this publication, he has a career batting average hovering around .300 (nearing the end of the 2019 season), four All-Star selections (2008, 2009, 2010, 2013), one Silver Slugger Award (2008), four Gold Glove Awards (2008, 2011, 2013, 2014), and was selected 2008 American League Most Valuable Player.

In addition to winning American League Rookie of the Year in 2007, he was integral to two team milestones that year. First, he made a diving stop on September 1 to preserve a no-hitter for fellow rookie Clay Bucholz against the Baltimore Orioles. The following month, he sealed Boston's World Series championship run in two crucial performances. The first was in game seven of the American League Championship Series against the Cleveland Indians, where he blasted a home run, a double and 5 RBIs to complete Boston's comeback from down three-games-to-one.

Then, leading off game one of the World Series against the Colorado Rockies, "Pedey" homered over Fenway Park's Green Monster, becoming only the second player ever (and the first rookie) to start the Fall Classic with a home run. Pedroia won a second World Series with Boston in 2013, a year after they finished dead last in their division, but barely saw action in their 2018 championship campaign due to injury. He is currently under contract to play for the Red Sox until 2021.

Pedroia is an avid believer of the legend of Bigfoot. In a January 2016 episode of Animal Planet's *Finding Bigfoot*, one contestant bet an autographed bat from Pedroia with another contestant on who would find more evidence of the creature's existence. Fittingly, the autograph read "Keep it Squashy," with an illustration of Sasquatch (aka Bigfoot) scrawled on the bottom of the bat. Pedroia himself, however, is far from a fan of the show, tweeting criticisms of it in 2013 for its lack of evidence and refusal to search for its namesake during the day. On his 30th birthday later that year on August 17, his teammates fittingly honored him with a Bigfoot cake.

40. R.J. REYNOLDS

Born in Sacramento in 1959, Robert James Reynolds attended Sacramento City College before being drafted by the Los Angeles Dodgers in the second round of the 1980 Amateur Draft. That selection marked a somewhat unlikely ascension through the sport, as Reynolds stopped playing high school baseball at Kennedy High School after his sophomore year. Yet three years later, he exploded as a walk-on for the SCC Panthers, hitting .455 with 40 RBIs in his only season with the team in 1980.

Dodgers scout and Sacramento native Ron King, two years removed from netting local great Steve Sax, was greatly impressed. After being drafted, Reynolds quickly matriculated through the Dodgers' farm system the next two years. Debuting as a September call-up for Los Angeles in 1983, he received mentorship from fellow Sacramento-bred baseball star Dusty Baker.

Baker, in his final year with Los Angeles, was frequently injured, creating playing opportunities for Reynolds down the stretch. And he made sure the hungry rookie made the most of them. "Baker used to talk to me all the time and more or less coach me along the way," Reynolds recounted the next year for the Sac City Express. "I'd go to hit, and he'd tell me about the pitchers... I learned a lot. He was like my teacher – or more or less like my big brother – and I was the pupil."

With that guidance, Reynolds' natural talent immediately made an impact. In his first game, he hit a three-run home run to power an 8-3 win over the San Diego Padres. That was just a warm-up for his biggest career highlight in a crucial game on September 11, against the Atlanta Braves at Dodger Stadium.

With Los Angeles and Atlanta locked in a battle for first place in the National League West, Reynolds stepped up to the plate in the bottom of the ninth inning with the bases loaded and the game tied at six following a Dodgers rally. He proceeded to lay down a perfect suicide squeeze bunt, scoring Pedro Guerrero from third and eliciting a famously exuberant call from announcer Vin Scully. "The Squeeze," as Scully termed it, gave Los Angeles a three-game lead in the NL West, which they went on to win by that margin.

Reynolds continued to suit up for the Dodgers until August of 1985, when he was traded to the Pittsburgh Pirates as part of a package to obtain slugger Bill Madlock. In the 1986 season opener, Reynolds commenced his first full year as a Pirate with a leadoff home run off New York Mets ace Dwight Gooden. Reynolds remained a solid player for Pittsburgh over the next few seasons, playing all three positions in the outfield and hitting for average. His steady contributions helped the Pirates reach the playoffs in 1990, where he appeared in all six games of the National League Championship Series against the Cincinnati Reds.

After 1990, Reynolds opted not to re-sign with the Pirates or another MLB team, instead playing baseball in Japan for three years before retiring at age 34.

Reynolds in his early days with the Los Angeles Dodgers.
Photo courtesy of the Sac City Express.

41. STEVE SAX

Born in West Sacramento on January 29, 1960, Stephen Louis Sax aspired to be a baseball star as early as age five. After five years in West Sacramento Little League and three in local Babe Ruth programs, he took the field for James Marshall High School (now River City High School). Despite struggling at the plate in his first year, he made the team again in his sophomore year due to a lack of infielders. It proved a blessing, as he hit .400 and was named to the All-City team, while James Marshall won the Golden Empire League championship.

Sax's junior year was even more superb, hitting .478 and breaking several school records. By the end of high school, he had earned All-American Honors in his junior and senior years, and the majors came calling fast. Renowned Los Angeles Dodgers scout Ron King flew into Sacramento from L.A. on a Friday afternoon in June 1978 and spent two-and-a-half hours negotiating a contract. Sax was then drafted by the Dodgers in that year's MLB Amateur Draft, spending the next three years in the minors before being called up to the majors late in the 1981 season.

Winning a World Series ring with the Dodgers that year, he quickly became their premiere second baseman, earning National League Rookie of the Year and an All-Star selection in 1982 thanks to a .282 batting average and 49 stolen bases. Despite gaining a reputation as a defensively erratic fielder the very next season with 30 errors (leading to the creation of the term "Steve Sax Syndrome" to describe a breakdown in a player's fielding mechanics), Sax's tenure with the Dodgers was especially fruitful. He earned two more All-Star appearances (1983, 1986), a Silver Slugger Award in 1986, and another World Series ring in 1988.

He followed that with three successful years for the New York Yankees, gaining two more All-Star selections (1989, 1990) and setting the team record for singles in a season (171) in 1989. Upon retirement in 1994, his career totals consisted of a .281 batting average, 1,949 hits and 444 stolen bases, having hit over .300 three times and stealing 40 or more bases six times.

Since retirement, Sax has been a multifaceted entrepreneur, working as a baseball analyst, financial consultant, martial artist, and even a candidate for the California State Assembly. Notably, he's made a number of cameos on television, most famously as himself (along with other contemporary MLB stars) in the classic 1992 *The Simpsons* episode "Homer at the Bat," widely considered one of the best in the show's long history. Sax was inducted into the Sacramento Sports Hall of Fame in 2014.

Sax attempting unsuccessfully to lay down a sacrifice bunt in game four of the 1988 World Series at the Oakland Coliseum in Oakland, CA. The Dodgers would go on to win the game 4-3, taking a 3-1 series lead over the Athletics. Photo taken by Eric Risberg, courtesy of the Associated Press.

42. NICK SWISHER

Born in Columbus, Ohio in 1980, Nicholas Thomas Swisher is the son of former MLB All-Star catcher Steve Swisher. While following in his father's footsteps by excelling at baseball in high school, Swisher initially made a bigger name for himself in football, even being recruited by the University of Notre Dame. Instead, he decided to dedicate his life to America's pastime, earning several Big Ten honors with the Ohio State Buckeyes baseball team. Swisher's selection by the Oakland Athletics in the 2002 MLB Amateur Draft was quickly immortalized in Michael Lewis's 2003 book *Moneyball*.

In 2004, Swisher punched his ticket to the majors thanks to a superb season with the River Cats. In 125 games, he roped 29 home runs and 92 RBIs alongside a .269 batting average, earning a promotion to the Athletics late in the season. Playing right field for all of 2005, Swisher blasted 21 home runs and 74 RBIs, placing sixth in American League Rookie of the Year voting as a result. His numbers jumped to 35 homers and 95 RBIs in 2006, helping Oakland advance to the American League Championship Series for the first time since 1990.

Swisher posing with a group of eager River Cats fans.
Photo courtesy of the Sacramento River Cats.

After another year donning the green and white, Swisher was traded to the Chicago White Sox in 2008. While his average dipped to an anemic .219, his 24 home runs helped Chicago win the American League Central Division title. Following the 2008 playoffs, he was traded once again to the New York Yankees, where he would enjoy his greatest spoils.

His 29 home runs and 82 RBIs in 2009 were part of New York's incredible offense, which powered its way to 103 wins and a World Series victory against the defending champion Philadelphia Phillies. The following year proved to be his finest regular season, hitting a career-high .288 and 29 home runs to earn his first All-Star selection.

After two more seasons in Yankee pinstripes, both ending with postseason trips, Swisher joined the Cleveland Indians as a free agent in December of 2012. Swisher knocked 22 homers and 63 RBIs in 2013, helping the Tribe reach 92 wins and a postseason berth a year after only winning 68 games. He boasts career totals of over 200 home runs and 1,300 hits in over a decade of play, in addition to hitting over 20 home runs in nine of his 11 full seasons in the majors. He retired from baseball in early 2017.

43. DAZZY VANCE

Charles Arthur "Dazzy" Vance was born in Orient, Iowa in 1891, and cultivated his baseball skills growing up in neighboring Nebraska. Pitching for various teams in the state, he managed to break through in the majors in 1915 with both the Pittsburgh Pirates and New York Yankees. However, he sustained an arm injury the following year, forcing him to head back to the minors for conditioning. The next few years witnessed Vance take the pitcher's mound for numerous minor league squads across the country, including the Sacramento Senators in 1919. That year, he won 10 games and spun a 2.82 ERA, but was stunted by arm injuries for a couple more years.

After tireless work proving himself in the minors, "Dazzy" finally found his way back to the majors in 1922 with the Brooklyn Robins (later the Dodgers). Right away, his persistence paid off, with 18 wins and a league-leading 134 strikeouts in 1922. Two years later in 1924, he amassed a season for the ages. He notched the pitching Triple Crown with 28 wins, 262 strikeouts and a 2.16 ERA, leading the National League in all three categories and subsequently winning the National League Most Valuable Player Award. Vance twirled a no-hitter the next season on September 13, 1925, against the Philadelphia Phillies, a year in which he led the National League in wins once again.

Perhaps his most remarkable feat, however, was leading the National League in strikeouts seven years in a row from 1922-1928. After a decade of brilliance with Brooklyn, Vance's skills began to decline in the early thirties, and he spent 1933 and 1934 bouncing between the St. Louis Cardinals and Cincinnati Reds. After years with also-ran teams in Brooklyn, he finally won a World Series with the 1934 "Gashouse Gang" Cardinals alongside future Solons manager Pepper Martin.

After a final season with the Dodgers in 1935, Vance retired with 197 wins, a career 3.24 ERA, 217 complete games, and 2,045 strikeouts, totals made all the more impressive given the arm injuries he overcame to even make it back to the majors. Vance's resilience was recognized in 1955 with induction into the Baseball Hall of Fame. He passed away six years later on February 16, 1961, in Homosassa Springs, FL.

44. GREG VAUGHN

Born in South Sacramento in 1965, Gregory Lamont Vaughn attended school locally at Kennedy High School and Sacramento City College before playing baseball at the University of Miami. He was selected in the first round of the 1986 MLB amateur draft by the Milwaukee Brewers, going on to play right field with them from 1989-1996, as well as the San Diego Padres (1996-1998), Cincinnati Reds (1999), Tampa Bay Devil Rays (2000-2002), and Colorado Rockies (2003). Despite generally low batting averages each season (usually around .250, his career average being .242), Vaughn made up for it with outstanding power. Finishing with 355 career homers and 1,072 RBIs, he had three seasons with at least 100 RBIs and four with 30 or more home runs.

1998 was by far his biggest year, earning National League Comeback Player of the Year, a trip to the World Series with the Padres, a Silver Slugger Award, and his second All-Star selection. In a bizarre twist, his 50 home runs that year, which would likely lead all of baseball in most seasons, placed a mere fourth behind Mark McGwire, Sammy Sosa and Ken Griffey Jr. Also an All-Star in 1993, 1996 and 2001, Vaughn is the cousin of fellow MLB slugger and contemporary Mo Vaughn. He was inducted into the Sacramento

Sports Hall of Fame in 2015, and remains active locally with celebrity golf tournaments and baseball clinics.

45. FERNANDO VINA

Born in Sacramento in 1969, Vina attended Valley High School in Elk Grove and Sacramento City College. He was a reliably consistent second base-man from 1993-2004, suiting up with the Seattle Mariners, New York Mets, Milwaukee Brewers, St. Louis Cardinals, and Detroit Tigers. Vina was selected to the 1998 All-Star Game with Milwaukee, and won Gold Glove Awards in 2001 and 2002 for the Cardinals. He also played in three consecutive post-seasons with St. Louis in 2000, 2001 and 2002, the first and third of which the club reached the National League Championship Series.

It was in no small part because of his consistently sound hitting, blasting a home run in game three of 2000 NLDS against Atlanta to help complete the sweep. In the 2002 NLDS against Arizona, he hit an incredible .600 to aid the Cardinals' sweep of the defending World Series champions. In addition to strong playoff performance, his relentless hitting and speed brought him the distinction of hitting the first inside-the-park home runs in both Oracle Park in San Francisco (May 9, 2000, when it was called Pacific Bell Park) and Miller Park in Milwaukee (October 2, 2001).

FUN FACTS

Vina starred in the music video for Jermaine Dupri's 2002 hit "Welcome to Atlanta (Coast 2 Coast Remix)," alongside the St. Lunatics and St. Louis Blues hockey player Fred Brathwaite.

46. JOHN VUKOVICH

Born in Sacramento on July 31, 1947, John Christopher Vukovich grew up in Sutter Creek and excelled as a ballplayer at Amador County High School. After attending American River College, he made a name for himself in the Pacific Coast League with the Eugene Emeralds (who later moved to Sacramento to become the new Solons in 1974). Throughout his MLB years, he worked tirelessly as a utility infielder with the Philadelphia Phillies (1970-1971 and 1976-1981), Milwaukee Brewers (1973-1974) and Cincinnati Reds (1975).

He was a member of two World Series championship teams, the 1975 Reds and 1980 Phillies, despite not making an appearance in a single post-season series. Nonetheless, he provided critical roster depth for both teams by backing up starters when necessary, one of the most important functions of a utility player. Despite his limited offensive statistics, "Vuke" was enormously popular in Philadelphia, endearing himself to Phillies teammates and fans with his blue-collar demeanor and tough approach to playing the game. Capable of playing all four infield positions, he was also an outstanding defender, with a career .951 fielding percentage. Phillies Hall of Famer Mike Schmidt, frequently hailed as the greatest third baseman in baseball history, later conceded that Vukovich was a much better defensive third baseman than him.

Following a brief managerial career, Vukovich made his biggest mark as a member of Philadelphia's coaching staff from 1988 to 2004, including bench coach for the club's improbable run to the World Series in 1993. Sadly, he passed away on March 8, 2007, from brain cancer. The Phillies subsequently recognized his far-reaching impact on the organization by inducting him into their Wall of Fame that August, before the team clinched its first postseason trip since 1993 the very next month.

47. WALLY WESTLAKE

Born in Gridley, CA, Waldon "Wally" Westlake was a graduate of Christian Brothers High School in Sacramento. His road to the majors was one fraught with adversity, even after signing with the Brooklyn Dodgers in 1940 at the tender age of 19. Initially suiting up for a minor league squad in Dayton, Ohio, Westlake struggled mightily at first. In his recollection to Ed Attanasio of *This Great Game*, he bluntly stated, "Every curveball fell off the table and I was a day late on every fastball...They called me into the front office one day, and gave me a pink slip and my bus ticket home. They told me I should go home, forget about baseball, because I'd never have the skills to be a professional ballplayer."

That night, en route to the bus that would take him out of town and away from his baseball dreams, he had a change of heart after passing by the brightly lit stadium. He recalled, "Forgive me, but the tears and the snot was flowing and I asked myself there: You think I am doing to quit? Not yet." Westlake stayed, and proceeded to advance through the minor leagues with the help of future Hall of Fame manager Casey Stengel.

Westlake sliding into third base as Jackie Robinson (who he finished behind in Rookie of the Year voting) covers. Photo courtesy of Alan O'Connor.

"He saved my butt," Westlake later said. "Called for me one day early in the season and said, 'You got talent, and you can catch and run well enough to play centerfield, but there's a lot more to it than just that. I am going to teach you how to play at the major league level.' And he did. For six months, he rode my biscuit, let me tell you...He taught me how to read the pitchers, how to anticipate in the field, so that I was in position to make the tricky catches."

It all paid off in his rookie year with the Pittsburgh Pirates in 1947, hitting .273 with 17 home runs and 69 RBIs. So outstanding was his rookie year that he was runner-up in Rookie of the Year voting to the one and only Jackie Robinson. He would go on to enjoy a career as a reliable journeyman with Pittsburgh (until the middle of the 1951 season), the St. Louis Cardinals (1951-1952), the Cincinnati Reds (1952), the Cleveland Indians (1952-1955), the Baltimore Orioles (1955), and the Philadelphia Phillies (1957).

Earning an All-Star selection in 1951, he's best known as a member of the 1954 Cleveland Indians, who won a then-record 111 regular season games and the American League pennant. Despite generally working as a utility player, Westlake nonetheless amassed highly respectable career totals of a .272 average, 127 homers and 539 RBIs. Westlake passed away in September 2019 at the age of 98.

48. JO-JO WHITE

Joyner Clifford "Jo-Jo" White was born in Red Oak, Georgia on June 1, 1909. Earning his nickname for the distinct way he pronounced the name of his home state, White became an outfielder, batting left-handed and throwing right-handed. After several years in the minors, he joined the Detroit Tigers early in 1932 as a centerfielder, in time to assist their pennant-winning teams a few years later in 1934 and 1935. In the 1934 season, White hit a resplendent .313, stole 28 bases and scored 97 runs. He followed it with a solid effort in the World Series against the "Gashouse Gang" St. Louis Cardinals, drawing eight walks and scoring six runs in Detroit's seven-game defeat.

White's batting average dipped to .240 in 1935, but he still managed to score 82 runs, steal 19 bases and hit 12 triples. In that year's World Series against the Chicago Cubs, "Jo-Jo" rose to the occasion once again. In the 11th inning of game three at Wrigley Field in Chicago, White roped an RBI single to give the Tigers a 6-5 victory, with the team clinching the first championship in franchise history three games later.

However, White's good times in Detroit came to an end in 1938. Frustrated by his shortened playing time in the past couple of seasons,

White (under the influence of several drinks) took out his anger on his manager, Del Baker, by ruining Baker's brand new felt hat.

As a result of his antics, he was promptly traded to the Seattle Rainiers of the Pacific Coast League, where he disciplined himself enough to win pennants in 1940 and 1941. Due to the talent depletion from major league players serving in World War II, Jo-Jo found his way back to the majors with the Philadelphia Athletics in 1943 and 1944, finishing with the Cincinnati Reds at the end of 1944.

Even with the door closed on his major league career, White still had significant capabilities as a player, which he would demonstrate with the Sacramento Solons. In 1945, he had the finest season of both his major and minor league careers in Sacramento, with 244 hits, 162 runs and a .355 batting average, all of which led the Pacific Coast League that season.

The remainder of his baseball career was spent primarily as a major league coach, working on the staffs of the Cleveland Indians (1958-1960), Detroit Tigers (1960), Kansas City Athletics (1961-1962), Milwaukee/Atlanta Braves (1963-1966), and Kansas City Royals (1969). He passed away on October 9, 1986, in Tacoma, Washington. In 1997, White was inducted posthumously into the Georgia Sports Hall of Fame.

49. VANCE WORLEY

Born in Sacramento in 1987, Vance Richard Worley attended McClatchy High School and Cal State Long Beach before being selected by the Philadelphia Phillies in the 2008 MLB Amateur Draft. After several call-ups in the latter half of 2010, Worley made his mark in the 2011 season, when the Phillies won 102 games and the National League East Division crown. While Philadelphia was predicted to be dominant, it was due to their starting rotation of Cliff Lee, Cole Hamels, Roy Halladay and Roy Oswalt; Worley seemed largely an afterthought compared to the "Four Horsemen."

However, he got the call to join the staff when Philadelphia's regular fifth starting pitcher, Joe Blanton, was injured in April. In his first start of 2011, he pitched six shutout innings, kicking off a stellar rookie season. He ended the year with an 11-3 record and a 3.01 ERA, finishing third in

National League Rookie of the Year voting behind Craig Kimbrel and Freddie Freeman.

After injury and control issues with the Phillies in 2012 and the Minnesota Twins in 2013, Worley re-established himself with the Pittsburgh Pirates, going 8-4 with a 2.85 ERA in 2014 and helping the Bucs reach the postseason for the second year in a row. He also contributed to another Pirates postseason trip in 2015, as well as one for the Baltimore Orioles in 2016.

50. BARRY ZITO

Originally from Las Vegas, Barry William Zito grew up in California with a mission to succeed in baseball. His family moved to San Diego to allow him to pursue a career in the game, with his father Joe even quitting work to help coach. Zito's parents weren't the only ones who dedicated themselves to mentoring him, as he received pitching tutoring from former San Diego Padre and 1976 Cy Young Award winner Randy Jones.

Jones had, to say the least, an effective way of keeping his protege in line when he made a mistake. "He would always spit his tobacco juice on my shoes," Zito recollected. "If I screwed up and made a bad pitch, he would sniper me from 5-6 feet out, right on my new shoes. And he didn't think twice about it."

After Grossmont High School in El Cajon and University of San Diego High School, Zito moved on to UC Santa Barbara, earning All-American Honors in his freshman year. Continuing to rack up honors and awards at Los Angeles Pierce College and University of Southern California, he passed up the chance to play for the Seattle Mariners and Texas Rangers to sign with the Oakland Athletics.

In 2000, starting the season with the Sacramento River Cats, he impressed with an 8-5 record, a 3.19 ERA and 91 strikeouts, quickly earning his major league debut in Oakland that July. Even with a late start, he immediately looked like an ace pitcher, finishing with seven wins and a 2.72 ERA, even out-pitching Yankees ace Roger Clemens in the playoffs.

Zito fires a pitch for the 2000 River Cats. Photo courtesy of the Sacramento River Cats.

A full season with the A's in 2001 yielded even greater fortune: a 17-8 record, 205 strikeouts and a league-leading 35 games started. 2002 witnessed Zito's finest regular season, with a 23-5 record, a 2.75 ERA and 182 strikeouts, enough to earn him the American League Cy Young Award. During this period, Zito gained enormous popularity as one of the three key starting pitchers (alongside Tim Hudson and Mark Mulder) of the revolutionary "Moneyball" A's teams.

He posted solid numbers for the next four seasons, his other career year in Oakland being 2006. Racking up 16 wins in 221 innings pitched, Zito outdueled Minnesota Twins ace Johan Santana in game one of the American League Division Series, helping Oakland advance past the first round of the playoffs after four heartbreaking consecutive ALDS exits beforehand.

Having ended his tenure with the Athletics on a resounding high note, Zito would next toe the rubber across the bay for the San Francisco Giants, signing a seven-year, $126 million contract in December of 2006, the most expensive contract ever given to a pitcher at the time. For the majority of his tenure in San Francisco, however, Zito was often derided as an expensive disappointment. He posted a losing record every year from 2007 through 2011, with his ERA never dipping below 4.00. Even when the team finally won its first World Series title in San Francisco in 2010, he was noted for having been left off the postseason roster all throughout October.

Then in 2012, nearing the end of his contract, Zito achieved a redemption tale for the ages. In the regular season, he totaled a superb 15-8 record as the Giants won 94 games and their second National League West Division title in three years. But his true rise from the ashes came in the National League Championship Series against the defending champion St. Louis Cardinals.

The Giants fell behind three-games-to-one, giving the Cardinals a chance to clinch the series at home in game five. After years of scorn for not performing up to his contract, Zito pitched the game of his life, shutting out St. Louis for 7⅔ innings and striking out six to send the series back to San Francisco.

The Giants would proceed to complete the comeback and advance to the World Series against the Detroit Tigers, where Zito allowed just one run in six innings as he outdueled Justin Verlander for a game one victory. It's all he would need to do, as San Francisco rolled to a sweep of Detroit for their second championship in three years. In a fitting swan song, he pitched the last game of his career for Oakland in September 2015 against San Francisco, opposite his former co-ace Tim Hudson.

Zito is currently pursuing a career in music, which he states he's "genuinely more in love" with than he ever was with baseball.

FUTURE STAR – RHYS HOSKINS

Following in the footsteps of Larry Bowa, John Vukovich and Brad Lidge, Rhys Dean Hoskins has emerged as another Sacramento star for the Philadelphia Phillies. A consummate local, he was born in the River City in 1993, and attended Jesuit High School before enrolling at Sacramento State University in 2011. Earning a selection in the 2014 MLB Draft by the Philadelphia Phillies, he made his debut in the 2017 season.

In an unforgettable MLB season that saw three teams win over 100 games, the Cleveland Indians win an American League record 22 games in a row, and rookie stars Aaron Judge and Cody Bellinger smash their respective league's rookie home run records, Hoskins made his own mark. Debuting on August 10, he hit his first home run just four days later in San Diego, en route to becoming the fastest player in major league history to reach 11 homers after their debut. He also became the first Phillies player to initiate a triple play from the outfield, and earned NL Rookie of the Month honors for August.

As of this publication, the Phillies are coming out of a rebuilding phase with hopes of returning to playoff contention, a mission boosted by signing superstar outfielder Bryce Harper to a record-setting 13-year contract in 2019. Much like Bowa, Vukovich and Lidge before him, Hoskins has a chance to bring the greatness of the River City to the City of Brotherly Love in a historic, lasting manner.

BONUS CHAPTER

RON KING – SACRAMENTO'S ALL-STAR SCOUT

Sacramento's century and a half of baseball heritage has produced a rich lineage of players, managers and coaches. Yet perhaps its most storied figure, despite only taking the field for a brief spell as a player and coach, excelled more when he surveyed it. His name was Ron King (Ronnie to his closest friends), a man whose life on the diamond spanned from Solons ball boy to minor league player to major league scout for the Pittsburgh Pirates and Los Angeles Dodgers. The way that life unfolded reads almost like the script for a classic Frank Capra film about baseball.

Like many baseball greats, he came from modest beginnings. Born into a Portuguese family in South Sacramento in 1928, King grew up an only child at 309 W St. near Southside Park. With no siblings, he was consumed by the national pastime right away. He carried a glove at all times, always eager for a session of catch with anyone he met. Dreaming of one day becoming a star player, he played in many local city league games to refine his skills.

All of these, of course, were typical components of a childhood love of baseball. But in 1937, King's zeal for the game led to an opportunity most boys his age could only dream of. He snagged a job as ball boy for the Sacramento Solons, when they had just entered their halcyon days as an affiliate in the St. Louis Cardinals' revered farm system. For 25 cents a game (35 cents for doubleheaders), King worked almost every facet of Cardinal Field until 1946. During this nine-year span, he climbed the stadium roof to gather foul balls, hung and lowered the flags in the outfield, tended to the home and visitor clubhouses, and worked the scoreboard. Downtime occasionally allowed for a session of catch with the players.

Yet this incredible experience almost didn't happen. A moment of youthful carelessness nearly cost King his coveted job, were it not for the intervention of a baseball luminary. Before one game, Solons president Phil Bartelme instructed King not to bring in the U.S. and California flags to his office after the game, as was his usual routine. The Solons won the game in 12 innings, which likely distracted King, who instinctively folded the flags and took them to Bartelme's office like always.

Instead of his boss, King found himself face to face with Cardinals executive Branch Rickey. Rickey's reputation as one of the sport's eminent geniuses wasn't lost on King, who stood aghast. "Wasn't that a great finish, young man?" Rickey politely asked the starstruck ball boy, who nervously replied, "Yes, sir." It was then that Bartelme came into the office for a meeting with Rickey, only to notice the unwanted presence of King and his folded flags. Rickey, no doubt sensing the prickly situation for his young acquaintance, quickly assured his colleague: "The boy and I were just discussing the game."

As it turned out, that wouldn't be the only time Rickey protected him. King returned to the office the next day, fully expecting to be fired by Bartelme, only to find the room empty. He trotted down to the field to open the gate on the first base side, where Rickey and Bartelme were standing nearby. Once again expecting a vicious reprimand from his boss, King instead heard Rickey shout across the field: "I hope the game tonight is as good as last night's, young man."

Sure enough, the verbal thrashing young Ronnie anticipated came that evening. Bartelme was straight with him: "He saved your bacon. I was going to fire you." It was nothing short of miraculous, being saved from certain firing not once, but twice by the man who pioneered the modern minor league farm system and later signed Jackie Robinson to break the MLB color barrier. Yet this wasn't the last charmed encounter Ron King had with a future Hall of Famer. Rather, it was merely the first.

Later in 1937, the PCL rival San Diego Padres were in town for a series. While tending to ball boy duties, King heard a fusillade of curse words streaming from the on-deck circle. He looked to see it came from an 18-year-old fellow named Ted Williams, who was mired in a bit of a hitting slump.

The lanky, left-handed slugger for San Diego was eyeing Solons pitcher Tony Freitas, hoping to launch a home run against Sacramento's ace southpaw. His first attempt to do so proved fruitless, as Freitas struck him out.

Williams cursed profusely as he trudged back to the dugout, tossing his bat and bitterly vowing to get the better of Freitas in his next at-bat. King placed his discarded bat on the rack, and his next time up, the "Splendid Splinter" uncorked a towering home run over the right field wall. The next day while playing catch with a Solons player, King remarked, "God, that guy can really swear!" To which the catcher replied, "Yeah kid, and he can really hit!" Williams, of course, would go on to become perhaps the finest pure hitter in baseball history for the Boston Red Sox.

After episodes like these, it was only fitting that King would be on hand for the Solons' miracle pennant clincher in 1942. Of course, he probably didn't expect it when that fateful last weekend of the season approached. The Los Angeles Angels came to town with a two-game lead over Sacramento, the Pacific Coast League pennant seemingly in hand. For Ronnie, it looked like just another weekend of clubhouse maintenance, gathering foul balls and adjusting the scoreboard.

On Saturday, with the Angels needing only one more win to secure the pennant, Los Angeles outfielder Arnold "Jigger" Statz was feeling especially confident. After going out to buy buckets of champagne for his club's seemingly inevitable celebration, Statz handed King some money and tasked him with fetching ice for the champagne. King swiftly did as requested, bolting up 4th and R Streets to purchase blocks of ice.

The Solons, however, had other plans. Recalled King: "The next day, they roped off the outfield...and right away in the first inning, Los Angeles hit a grand slam home run, and most of the people were saying, 'They lost those games on purpose to draw a good crowd on Sunday!' So a couple home runs and Sacramento gets back in the game. Ray Mueller, who was the most valuable player in the league, hits a home run, I think it was in the eighth. And they brought on Tony Freitas, who had pitched two games already, relieved in that game for the save. And then he started in the second game and shut Los Angeles out."

The iced champagne that seemed a guarantee for Los Angeles was swiftly moved over to the home clubhouse by King. He wasn't paid much for his efforts, but that was more than compensated by the joy of his hometown team's storybook first pennant. "Winning the pennant was something the city never had," King later said. "They never had anything."

As childhood gave way to adolescence, King's baseball ambitions expanded beyond gathering foul balls at Cardinal Field. He began attending Christian Brothers High School, located mere blocks away from his dream job. Unsurprisingly, he quickly gained a reputation as the school's resident baseball guru, as encapsulated by a 1946 page of the school newspaper that read: "Do you want to know anything about baseball? Ask Ronnie King." That same year, he was named to *The Sacramento Union*'s All-City Team. At age 15, he became the youngest player ever to participate in the National Division. His success wasn't limited to just baseball, playing football in his freshman and sophomore years and becoming student body vice president in his senior year.

After a magical childhood with the Solons and all-star success in high school, King was set to fulfill his dream of excelling in the professional ranks. In 1943, a scout from the New York Yankees offered to sign King. But when his father learned he'd be playing minor league ball across the country in Norfolk, Virginia, the deal was called off, fearing for his son's safety in case the U.S. lost World War II. He wouldn't have to wait long, as the Cleveland Indians came calling in 1946, the year after the war came to an end.

If King's life were indeed the subject of a classic baseball movie, the next chapter would have him tearing up the minors en route to major league stardom. It seemed like the perfectly scripted chapter to follow the previous ones: working Cardinal Field during the Solons' glory years, having his job saved by Branch Rickey, handing a budding Ted Williams the bat for a slump-busting home run, being front and center for his hometown team's miracle pennant run, and making all-city honors as a high school player.

But this was real life, not the movies, and King's professional career didn't pan out in the idyllic fashion it should have. For the next ten years, King flitted around various minor league circuits. He played in Class C Billings, Montana in 1948, hitting .303, and won a Central League Class AA championship with Dayton, Ohio the following year. Like many players (including childhood acquaintance Ted Williams), he enlisted in the Armed Forces during the Korean War from 1950 to 1953.

Upon returning from service in Korea, King was sent to Cleveland's single-A club in Reading, Pennsylvania, where he would suit up with future major leaguers Joe Altobelli, Rocky Colavito and Bud Daley. However, even at age 25, his eyesight was beginning to deteriorate. In 1954, he left the Cleveland organization to play for his hometown Sacramento Solons for 30 games. But while playing for a Class A team in Salem, Oregon, he suffered a slipped disc while sliding into second. It marked the end of his playing career shortly thereafter.

With his playing days behind him, King seemed headed for a normal life. He began working in education before welcoming the birth of his daughter Toni. With a steady job and the onset of family life, the dream of major league stardom from his youth was officially over. But as it turned out, he wouldn't need a single at-bat in the majors to leave his mark there. In 1960, Pittsburgh Pirates general manager Joe L. Brown contacted King with the golden opportunity of becoming a scout for the team.

It wasn't a glamorous position that would earn him stardom, nor put his likeness on a Topps card. But Brown had a unique way of pitching it: "The streetcar only comes by every so often, so if you want to be a scout, you better get on the streetcar." King was persuaded and joined Pittsburgh, scouring the greater Sacramento area for prime talent.

For many fans, scouts rarely (if ever) come to mind when following their favorite team. A scout's work is entirely behind the scenes, and they generally don't receive scrutiny from fans the same way players, coaches, general managers and owners do. The prevalent image one might conjure of a scout is a relatively leisurely one, of middle-aged men with straw hats and Hawaiian shirts gripping radar guns and quietly taking notes as they watch a game.

Yet the life of a baseball scout can be every bit as demanding as that of a player. To be a successful scout, one must possess an expertise of the game nothing short of top-tier. King drew upon one of the greatest baseball minds ever (and the man who saved his ball boy job), Branch Rickey, to best approach scouting. Rickey's philosophy was simple: speed comes first, everything else is secondary. He also had a constant helping hand at his side in his wife, Betty, who earned the nickname "Betty Gun" for all the times she held a speed gun to gauge a pitcher's fastball.

Additionally, some scouts travel farther than most players in a given year. "I always thought baseball, for me, was quite an education," King later recalled to historian William Burg. "I went all over the country, I went to Canada, Puerto Rico, the Dominican and all those other places." For an eight-year span, Ron and Betty would fly to Hawaii during winter to scout for up to six weeks. In addition to globetrotting in search of promising talent, King would also venture into local neighborhoods few other scouts would tread. Even if it was a rough area torn by racial strife, like that of Sacramento High School, King still went to find the right player.

King spent 14 years with the Pirates, during which they won two World Series titles in 1960 and 1971. During the 1971 series against Baltimore, Ron and Betty had the pleasure of taking in the first ever night World Series game at Three Rivers Stadium in Pittsburgh. An even bigger opportunity came calling in 1974. Al Campanis, general manager of the Los Angeles Dodgers, approached King with a scouting position that would pay $300 more than his current one with Pittsburgh. The Pirates were unwilling to match L.A.'s offer and released him from his contract.

King enjoyed continued success during his time with Los Angeles. The Dodgers went to the World Series four times (1974, 1977, 1978 and 1981) during that span, winning it in 1981, and King and his fellow scouts were invited to attend the games. They even received rings every time the Dodgers won a pennant or championship, while their wives were given pendants. Owner Walter O'Malley treated them handsomely, even once taking them all to Hawaii for a week.

Ron King certainly earned such leisure given his work as a scout. He discovered and developed many notable players, such as R.J. Reynolds (who lifted the Dodgers to the playoffs in 1983 with his famous walk-off suicide squeeze) and outfielder Rudy Law, who would later enjoy his greatest success in the ALCS for the 1983 Chicago White Sox. His greatest move was signing West Sacramento native Steve Sax in 1978, who became an All-Star second baseman that helped the Dodgers win two World Series titles in the '80s.

However, King's time with the Dodgers came to an end in 1987 amidst a tumultuous time for the franchise. In the same year that marked the 40th anniversary of Jackie Robinson's debut, Campanis made racially insensitive remarks during an interview with Ted Koppel on ABC's *Nightline* and was subsequently fired. King's contract expired, and he continued his scouting career working for the Phillies for several years.

In 1991, he returned to Pittsburgh and scouted players like All-Star catcher Jason Kendall for the next nine years. His decades of fruitful scouting were recognized in 1997, when Major League Baseball honored him as West Coast Scout of the Year. The award served as the much-deserved apogee to his career, retiring shortly thereafter in 2000, a full 40 years after he accepted Joe L. Brown's once-in-a-lifetime offer.

King's magnificent story came to an end on October 26, 2015, dying peacefully in his sleep at age 87 at his home in Land Park. His passing was met with fond remembrances and praise from former colleagues and players he scouted. "He was like a second father to me," said Steve Sax. "He was a tutor to a lot of players, an unbelievable man. He knew just about everything in baseball." "A baseball encyclopedia - that was Ronnie," added former Solons and Chicago Cubs catcher Cuno Barragan. "Ask him about any player, and he knew something about them."

Looking back on his life with writer Rick Cabral in 2010, five years before his passing, King realized with gratitude how much scouting and playing had led to a fulfilling life. "I really had a good time," he said. Given his work with two of MLB's most renowned franchises, and a lifetime of connection to Sacramento baseball from Solons ball boy to signing major league stars, it's a baseball life most could only dream of living.

BIBLIOGRAPHY

Androvich, Bob and James, Will. *Baseball Comes Home: The Magic of Raley Field and the Sacramento River Cats' Premiere Season*. Sacramento: Circus Catch Publishing, 2000. Print.

Armstrong, L. (2010, October 14). Sacramento's Ron King reminisces about lifelong love for baseball. *Valley Community Newspapers*. Retrieved from *http://www.valcomnews.com/?p=1925*

Attanasio, E. They Were There: Wally Westlake [Blog post]. Retrieved from *http://www.thisgreatgame.com/wally-westlake.html*

Baillie, S. (1957, May 30). PCL to Battle Major Switch. *The Desert Sun*. Retrieved from *https://cdnc.ucr.edu/?a=d&d=DS19570530.2.51&srpos=2&e=-------en--20--1--txt-txIN-fred+david+solons-------1*

Banner Year For Sacramento Club Predicted in 1937. (1936, July 30). *Calexico Chronicle*, p. 5. Retrieved from *https://cdnc.ucr.edu/?a=d&d=CC19360730.2.57&srpos=1&e=-------en--20--1--txt-txIN-branch+rickey+sacramento-------1*

Bedingfield, G. (2008, May 28). Gene Bearden [Blog post]. Retrieved from *http://www.baseballinwartime.com/player_biographies/bearden_gene.htm*

Cabral, R. (2010, April 16). A Life Fit for a King [Blog post]. Retrieved from *http://www.baseballsacramento.com/Spotlight-Ronnie_King,SuperScout.html*

---. (2011, May 25). Wally Westlake and the 1954 World Series [Blog post]. Retrieved from *http://www.baseballsacramento.com/History-Travelin'_1954.html*

Connell, S. (1974, January 10). The Camellia Bowl – Sacto blows it again. *The Express*, p. 11. Retrieved from *https://cdnc.ucr.edu/?a=d&d=EXP19740110.1.11&srpos=2&e=-------197-en--20--1-byDA-txt-txIN-sacramento+solons+hughes+stadium-------1*

Crasnick, J. (2016, April 19). AL MVP Josh Donaldson still sees himself as an underdog [Blog post]. Retrieved from *https://www.espn.com/mlb/story/_/id/15229047/josh-donaldson-not-resting-mvp-laurels*

Cutter, W. (1922, February 4). Sacramento's New $75,000 Ball Park Nearing Completion. *The Sacramento Union*, p. 5. Retrieved from *https://cdnc.ucr.edu/cgi-bin/cdnc?a=d&d=SU19220204.2.56&e=-------en--20--1--txt-txIN--------1*

Damaged fence upsets Solons. (1976, May 13). *The Express*, p. 1. Retrieved from *https://cdnc.ucr.edu/?a=d&d=EXP19760513.1.1&srpos=27&e=-------197-en--20--21-byDA-txt-txIN-sacramento+solons+hughes+stadium-------1*

Deadline 3 P.M., Where is Moreing With Cash? (1934, February 13). *Oakland Tribune*, p. 18. Retrieved from *https://cdnc.ucr.edu/?a=d&d=OT19340213.1.18&srpos=8&e=-------en--20--1--txt-txIN-moreing+field+lights-------1*

Engelmann, L. (1987, October 26). WHEN GIANTS WALKED THE EARTH: Barnstorming With Gehrig and the Babe. *The Los Angeles Times*. Retrieved from *http://articles.latimes.com/1987-10-26/sports/sp-11011_1_babe-ruth/3*

Fritz, A. (1976, February 5). Touching the Bases - Baker, Lee: hometown talent. *The Express*, p. 11. Retrieved from *https://cdnc.ucr.edu/?a=d&d=EXP19760205.1.11&srpos=12&e=-------en--20--1--txt-txIN-dusty+baker-------1*

Grimes May Manage Solons. (1938, November 14). *The Healdsburg Tribune and Enterprise*, p. 2. Retrieved from *https://cdnc.ucr.edu/?a=d&d=HTES19381114.2.22&srpos=4&e=-------en--20--1--txt-txIN-Solons+baseball-------1*

Gurnick, K. (2015, October 30). Dodgers scout King, 87, passes away. *MLB*. Retrieved from *https://www.mlb.com/news/dodgers-scout-ron-king-dies/c-156001358*

Gutierrez, A. (2019, May 20). Dusty Baker recalls Hank Aaron's mentorship, how high five was created [Interview transcript]. NBC Sports Bay Area. Retrieved from *https://www.nbcsports.com/bayarea/giants/dusty-baker-recalls-hank-aarons-mentorship-how-high-five-was-created*

J. I. Taylor of Boston to Buy Interest in Senators. (1910, January 9). *The Sacramento Union*, p. 12. Retrieved from *https://cdnc.ucr.edu/?a=d&d=SU19100109.2.89&srpos=5&e=-------en--20--1--txt-txIN-john+i.+taylor+senators+baseball-------1*

King, R. (2007, April 6). Interview by W. Burg, audio recording.

Kruse, Jeff. "A Minor League Baseball Flyer That Tells It Like It Is." *Mad Magazine*. August 2014: p. 45.

Ladson, B. (2016, October 5). Set to face Dodgers, Dusty reflects on trade to LA. *MLB*. Retrieved from *https://www.mlb.com/news/dusty-baker-reflects-on-trade-to-dodgers/c-205075404*

Lindsley, J. (1944, February 23). Sacramento Fans Save Franchise. *San Pedro News-Pilot*, p. 10. Retrieved from *https://cdnc.ucr.edu/?a=d&d=SPNP19440223.2.133&srpos=4&e=-------en--20--1--txt-txIN-dick+edmonds+yubi+separovich-------1*

Martinez, Buck. *From Worst to First: The Toronto Blue Jays in 1985*. Toronto: Fitzhenry and Whiteside, 1985. Print.

Matsui, Doris. "In Honor of the 2007 Sacramento River Cats." Speech, Washington, DC, October 16, 2007. Congressional Record. Retrieved from *https://www.congress.gov/congressional-record/2007/10/16/extensions-of-remarks-section/article/E2145-3*.

McDermott, Mark. *Touching All the Bases: A Look at the Players, Teams and Leagues That For More Than 100 Years Have Made the Sacramento Area a Hotbed for Baseball Talent*. Sacramento: 2017. Print.

Murrieta, E. (1984, September 27). Reynolds: The new 'Natural.' *Sac City Express*, p. 6. Retrieved from *https://cdnc.ucr.edu/?a=d&d=EXP19840927.1.6&srpos=1&e=-------en--20--1--txt-txIN-r.j.+reynolds+express+baseball-------1*

Nava, J. (1975, April 3). Rape declines at City during last four years. *The Express*, p. 3. Retrieved from *https://cdnc.ucr.edu/?a=d&d=EXP19750403.1.3&srpos=12&e=-------en--20--1--txt-txIN-hughes+stadium+solons+parking-------1*

Newland, R. (1935, June 11). Scouting Western Sports. *Calexico Chronicle*, p. 4. Retrieved from *https://cdnc.ucr.edu/?a=d&d=CC19350611.2.62&srpos=2&e=-------en--20--1--txt-txIN-lew+moreing-------1*

Night students fight pro baseball parking. (1974, February 28). *The Express*, p. 1. Retrieved from *https://cdnc.ucr.edu/?a=d&d=EXP19740228.1.1&srpos=7&e=------197-en--20--1-byDA-txt-txIN-sacramento+solons+baseball-------1*

Nishimura, S. (1978, June 14). Dodgers Pick Steve Sax. *News-Ledger*, p. 1. Retrieved from *https://cdnc.ucr.edu/?a=d&d=WSN19780614.2.3&srpos=3&e=-------en--20--1--txt-txIN-ron+king+baseball+scout-------1*

O'Connor, Alan. *Gold on the Diamond: Sacramento's Greatest Baseball Players, 1886-1976*. Sacramento: Big Tomato Press, 2008. Print.

Pardee Will Pitch. (1903, March 26). *Los Angeles Herald*, p. 4. Retrieved from *https://cdnc.ucr.edu/?a=d&d=LAH19030326.2.79&srpos= 4&e=------190-en--20--1--txt-txIN-mike+fisher+sacramento+baseball-------1*

Paris, J. (2013, April 27). One backyard, two Cy Young Awards. *The San Diego Union-Tribune*. Retrieved from *https://www.sandiegouniontribune.com/ sports/mlb/sdut-barry-zito-randy-jones-2013apr27-story.html*

Perlstein, Rick. *The Invisible Bridge: The Fall of Nixon and the Rise of Reagan*. New York: Simon & Schuster, 2014. Print.

Pete. (1920, October 29). Mails Receives Most Gigantic Welcome Ever Given Athlete Here. *The Sacramento Union*, p. 8. Retrieved from *https://cdnc.ucr.edu/?a=d&d =SU19201029.2.86&srpos=8&e=-------en--20--1--txt-txIN-walter+mails+parade-------1*

Plaschke, B. (1987, August 18). A New Career of Providing Relief: Former Padre Metzger Is Still Called for Help; Now Fights Real Fires. *The Los Angeles Times*. Retrieved from *http://articles.latimes.com/1987-08-18/sports/ sp-2207_1_butch-metzger*

Poole, D. (1975, December 3). Recollections and Observations. *News-Ledger*, p. 2. Retrieved from *https://cdnc.ucr.edu/?a=d&d=WSN19751203.2.8&srpos=16 7&e=------197-en--20--161-byDA-txt-txIN-great+american+freedom+train+sac ramento-------1*

Rinehart, G. (1974, February 14). Mayor officially welcomes Solons. *The Express*, p. 8. Retrieved from *https://cdnc.ucr.edu/cgi-bin/ cdnc?a=d&d=EXP19740214.1.8&e=-------en--20--1--txt-txIN--------1*

Rodgers, D. (Producer and writer). (2006). *KCRA* [Television Series]. Sacramento, CA: KCRA-3.

Ryll, Erich D. (2011). A 30-Year Historic Review of a Community Hospital Epidemic Outbreak Characterized by Venous Inflamma. *International Association for Chronic Fatigue Syndrome/Myalgic Encephalomyelitis*. Retrieved from *http://iacfsme.org/ME-CFS-Primer-Education/Bulletins/ BulletinRelatedPages/A-30-Year-Historic-Review-of-a-Community-Hospital/ A-30-Year-Historic-Review-of-a-Community-Hospital.aspx*

Sacramento Club Sale is Blocked. (1944, February 14). *Madera Daily Tribune*, p. 2. Retrieved from *https://cdnc.ucr.edu/?a=d&d=MT19440214.2.32&srpos=47&e=-------en--20--41--txt-txIN-Solons+baseball-------1*

Sacramento Hurler Bags Coast Record. (1939, August 18). *Calexico Chronicle*, p. 4. Retrieved from *https://cdnc.ucr.edu/?a=d&d=CC19390818.2.59&srpos=89&e=-------en--20--81--txt-txIN-Solons+baseball-------1*

Schoenfield, D. (2012, September 5). The greatest play ever made. *ESPN*. Retrieved from *http://www.espn.com/blog/sweetspot/post/_/id/28631/the-greatest-play-ever-made*

Shenk, L. (2017, March 8). Remembering John Vukovich [Blog post]. Retrieved from *https://philliesinsider.mlblogs.com/remembering-john-vukovich-d6d1e966e854*

Smith, Ron. *Heroes of the Hall*. St. Louis: The Sporting News, 2002. Print.

Solons Win Night Game. (1930, June 11). *The Colusa Herald*, p. 2. Retrieved from *https://cdnc.ucr.edu/?a=d&d=CSH19300611.2.29&srpos=1&e=-------en--20--1--txt-txIN-moreing+field+lights-------1*

Solon to Offer Riches to Rags. (1943, March 22). *Madera Tribune*, p. 1. Retrieved from *https://cdnc.ucr.edu/?a=d&d=MT19430322.2.17&srpos=1&e=-------en--20--1--txt-txIN-1942+sacramento+solons+-------1*

Spalding, John E. *Sacramento Senators and Solons: Baseball in California's Capital, 1886 to 1976*. Manhattan: Ag Press, 1995. Print.

Stark, Jayson. *Worth the Wait: Tales of the 2008 Phillies*. Chicago: Triumph Books, 2009. Print.

Stevenson, M. (1974, April 25). Solons opener brightens City College night life. *The Express*, p. 9. Retrieved from *https://cdnc.ucr.edu/?a=d&d=EXP19740425.1.9&srpos=10&e=-------en--20--1--txt-txIN-bob+lemon+solons-------1*

"Studio Sacramento: Greg Vaughn." *Studio Sacramento*. PBS. KVIE, Sacramento. 23 Mar. 2012. Television.

"The Golden Game – Baseball in Sacramento." *ViewFinder*. PBS. KVIE, Sacramento. 21 Mar. 2008. Television.

Tom Jefferson still survives. (1976, May 6). *The Express*, p. 4. Retrieved from *https://cdnc.ucr.edu/?a=d&d=EXP19760506.1.4&srpos=2&e=-------en--20--1--txt-txIN-maury+wills+hughes+stadium+bump-------1*

United Press. (1939, March 11). Solons Have No Pep, Says Branch Rickey. *The San Bernardino Sun*, p. 14. Retrieved from *https://cdnc.ucr.edu/?a=d&d=SBS1939 0311.1.14&srpos=24&e=------193-en--20--21-byDA.rev-txt-txIN-branch+rickey+ sacramento-------1*

United Press International. (1974, August 17). Dunning Tosses First No-Hitter. *The Desert Sun*, p. A6. Retrieved from *https://cdnc.ucr.edu/?a=d&d=DS19740817. 2.61&srpos=5&e=-------en--20--1--txt-txIN-solons+hughes+stadium-------1*

---. (1974, August 21). Phoenix Home of Single. *The Desert Sun*, p. B3. Retrieved from *https://cdnc.ucr.edu/?a=d&d=DS19740821.2.119&srpos= 1&e=-------en--20--1--txt-txIN-solons+gorman+thomas-------1*

Valdez, J. (2015, December 9). How former Panthers baseball player Larry Bowa made it to the MLB. *The Express*. Retrieved from *http://saccityexpress.com/ how-former-panthers-baseball-player-larry-bowa-made-it-to-the-mlb/*

Vaughn, B. (1948, July 12). Fire ravages Solons' home in 1948. *The Sacramento Bee*. Retrieved from *https://www.sacbee.com/news/local/history/ article160863534.html*

Velotta, V. (2018, September 27). Retired All-Star Closer Brad Lidge is a Freaking Archaeologist Now [Blog post]. Retrieved from *https://www.12up.com/posts/ 6182473-retired-all-star-closer-brad-lidge-is-a-freaking-archaeologist-now*

Vistica, D. (2014, July 1). Personal interview.

Watson Jr., L. (2009, April 21). Forgotten Stories of Courage and Inspiration: Gene Bearden [Blog post]. Retrieved from *https://bleacherreport.com/ articles/160125-forgotten-stories-of-courage-and-inspiration-gene-bearden*

Weisman, J. (2013, September 11). A Happier 9/11 [Blog post]. Retrieved from *https://www.dodgerthoughts.com/2013/09/11/a-happier-911-2/*

What Taylor Has Been to Senators. (1910, March 3). *The Sacramento Union*, p. 8. Retrieved from *https://cdnc.ucr.edu/?a=d&d=SU19100303.2.76&srpos= 2&e=-------en--20--1--txt-txIN-john+i.+taylor+senators+baseball-------1*

Williams, M. (1978, October 26). Hughes throws birthday party; Solons were crammed. *The Express*, p. 8. Retrieved from *https://cdnc.ucr. edu/?a=d&d=EXP19781026.1.8&e=-------en--20--1--txt-txIN-1976+sacramento+ solons+baseball-------1*

INDEX

ACKNOWLEDGMENTS

The number of people to whom I owe a debt of gratitude for this book is seemingly infinite. Nonetheless, I intend to acknowledge them all, as it's the least I can do in light of the publication of a first book I am very proud of.

First is the wonderful Alan O'Connor, the dean of Sacramento baseball history. His cooperation in giving me many great pictures ensured this project could attain the quality I aspired to. His excellent book *Gold on the Diamond* covers a lot of players I wasn't able to here, and I highly recommend everyone read it. Equal gratitude goes to the River Cats and Sac City Express for providing additional photos. Former River Cats executive Dan Vistica is also much appreciated for letting me interview him in his office in the summer of 2014.

I also must acknowledge other Sacramento baseball historians past and present like John E. Spalding, Rick Cabral, Mark McDermott, Frances Pendleton, William McPoil, and William Shubb, among others. Without their work, my efforts would have taken far longer.

Eternal thanks go to my parents, Bill and Bonnie. I couldn't possibly gauge the time they spent providing crucial input, as well as editing. Whether it was mom editing or dad coming up with great ideas on how to flesh out certain passages, they were indispensable. Thanks also to sister Morgan for helping Dad and I take some great pictures downtown of the sites of old stadiums.

Of course, this book wouldn't exist without my board colleagues at the Sacramento Historical Society. Greg Voelm got it rolling by hiring me as an intern to start it. William Burg provided his 2007 audio interview with Ron King. Gregg Lukenbill was clutch in securing the Knights of Columbus Hall for my April 2018 presentation of this book's subject matter for the society. Steve Beck had me as a guest for a Sac baseball episode of Access Sacramento's *Living in the West*.

Thanks also to the splendid Jonathan Daniel, who runs the outstanding blog '80s Baseball. In August 2017, I came into contact with Jonathan and he asked if I'd like to do a feature post about Larry Bowa's significance to both Sacramento and Philadelphia. I did so, and it ultimately made the passage about him here much stronger.

Likewise, I'd like to acknowledge my colleagues at Dodgers Nation: Gary Lee, Brook Smith, Clint Pasillas, Clint Evans, Tim Rogers, AJ Gonzalez, Daniel Preciado, Blake Williams, Zed Santiago, Brian Robitaille, Hillary Thompson, Tamara Issi, Jason McClure, Megan Garcia, Kellan Grant, Doug McKain, and others. They have given me a chance to grow as a baseball writer the way I've always dreamed. That was especially crucial in improving this book in its final stages of completion.

I also must take a moment to thank some of my best "baseball friends." I'm not talking about friends who just like the game...I'm talking about the bleedings hearts types that understand it's *more* than a game. First is the Angry Twins Fan family: Brad, Kevin, John, Cameron, Sandi, Keith, PJ, Jonathan, and others. Next are my 1864 base ball friends, who I shall refer to by their player nicknames: Brandywine, Chesty, Crash, Blackjack, Pops, Kraken, Bat Man, Mailman, Teach, The Hammer, and many others. All of these friends have helped in affirming the depth and vitality of my love of baseball, thus realizing how seriously I should take it. If this book existed without that, it certainly wouldn't be as good.

ABOUT THE AUTHOR

Born in Orange County in 1989, Marshall Garvey has been an avid baseball fan and historian since 2000. His writing has been published by *The Sacramento Bee*, Dodgers Nation, '80s Baseball, Richard Nixon Foundation, Teen Ink Magazine, and the Sacramento Historical Society. He runs the popular Sacramento-based video game site Last Token Gaming, which celebrated its sixth anniversary in June 2019. His popular Dodgers Nation article "Letter from a Fan: Life, Death, and the 2017 Los Angeles Dodgers" received widespread praise, including from *Sports Illustrated* writer Jon Weisman and former Dodgers catcher Kyle Farmer.

In 2010, he created the Presidents Baseball educational card franchise, which cleverly envisions all 45 U.S. Presidents as members of their own baseball team. A graduate of UC Davis in 2014 with a B.A. in history, he currently works as a full-time history book author and consultant. He also serves on the board of directors for the Sacramento Historical Society. His hobbies include jogging, going to the movies, collecting music, attending concerts, boxing, studying history, video games, and playing 1864 base ball with friends.